INVESTING
WITH THE
HEDGE FUND
GIANTS

INVESTING
WITH THE
HEDGE FUND
GIANTS

Profit Whether Markets
Rise or Fall

BEVERLY CHANDLER

FINANCIAL TIMES
PITMAN PUBLISHING

FINANCIAL TIMES

MANAGEMENT

LONDON · SAN FRANCISCO
KUALA LUMPUR · JOHANNESBURG

*Financial Times Management delivers the knowledge,
skills and understanding that enable students,
managers and organisations to achieve their ambitions,
whatever their needs, wherever they are.*

London Office:
128 Long Acre, London WC2E 9AN
Tel: +44 (0)171 447 2000
Fax: +44 (0)171 240 5771
Website: www.ftmanagement.com

A Division of Financial Times Professional Limited

First published in Great Britain in 1998

The right of Beverly Chandler to be identified as
author of this work has been asserted by her in accordance
with the Copyright, Designs and Patents Act 1988.

ISBN 0 273 63243 4

British Library Cataloguing in Publication Data
A CIP catalogue record for this book can be obtained from
the British Library.

1 3 5 7 9 10 8 6 4 2

Typeset by Northern Phototypesetting Co Ltd, Bolton
Printed and bound in Great Britain by
Biddles Ltd, Guildford and King's Lynn

*The Publishers' policy is to use paper manufactured
from sustainable forests.*

ABOUT THE AUTHOR

Beverly Chandler is an investment writer of some 12 years standing. This is her third investment book. She was founder and editor of *Managed Derivatives* magazine, and organizer of the magazine's associated conferences. She has also been the European editor of the International Herald Tribune's *International Fund Investment* and the European Associate Editor for *MAR/Hedge*.

During her career she has worked as a freelance financial journalist for most of the financial press in the UK. In 1993, Beverly won the Rose-Baratz Journalism Award. Latterly, Beverly has been writing almost exclusively about alternative investment management.

Beverly is married with two children and lives on the Isle of Wight.

CONTENTS

PREFACE

At the time of publication, the state of the markets has overtaken some of the examples in this book. For the record, the events of August 1998, when the Russian market collapsed and caused turmoil in the rest of the investing world, have had their effect on hedge funds.

It is still not clear what losses have been sustained, but *MAR/Hedge* reports from figures available that short sellers had a field day with an average gain of 21.8 per cent over the month while global managers, in whose sector *MAR/Hedge* includes the emerging market funds, lost 8.8 per cent with the emerging market sub-set losing 21.0 per cent. Some of the most successful fund management groups for a number of years, including, sadly Everest Capital (interviewed in Chapter Six), had their worst month of performance ever, with losses estimated at over 30 per cent.

Emerging markets, with their lack of liquidity and infrastructure can be the most volatile of markets. In the case of Russia, not many investors expected a default on short-term debt, a moratorium on banks and companies repaying debts and a devaluation of the rouble on the same day. Given those events happening, traditional hedging techniques – which were hard to come by in these markets in the best of times – became worthless, hence the severity of the losses. The system is paralysed and many emerging market fund managers are unable, even now, to estimate the net asset value of their funds.

There are winners in this dismal market scenario and in this case, these are the market neutral hedge fund managers who lived up to their aim of achieving performance independently of the markets and stayed fairly flat, reporting a gain of 0.40 per cent while the stock markets recorded significant losses. All this goes to demonstrate the complexity of the hedge fund sector, a characteristic which only makes it the more interesting.

Beverly Chandler
September 1998

INTRODUCTION

Hedge funds are largely misunderstood. There is no simple definition of a hedge fund and no two hedge funds are the same. The
name refers to a whole sector of investment
and, despite the hype, it is not a sector that is
entirely new. When I mentioned to a friend
who works in the City of London that I was
writing a book on hedge funds, she said: "But
they're just a marketing ploy, aren't they?"
And in many ways she is right. The aura of mystique and mystery that
has grown around hedge funds is a useful marketing ploy – and as
scoundrels and marketing managers know there is nothing like
making something sound dangerous for attracting investors.

> **"There is no simple
> definition of a hedge fund
> and no two hedge funds
> are the same."**

Source: Rostron Parry

Explaining the hedge fund

But in reality, hedge funds are continuing the work that active investment managers have always undertaken – since the start of trading on
a commercial scale and the rise of capitalism in Europe, particularly
in the Netherlands and the UK, in the 17th century. Writing about this

in *Against the Gods*, Peter L Bernstein sums up the new freedoms that money brought.

> The second half of the 17th century was also an era of burgeoning trade. The Dutch were the predominant commercial power of the time, and England was their main rival. Ships arrived daily from colonies and suppliers around the globe to unload a profusion of products that had once been scarce or unknown luxuries – sugar and spice, coffee and tea, raw cotton and fine porcelain. Wealth was no longer something that had to be inherited from preceding generations: now it could be earned, discovered, accumulated, invested – and protected from loss.

In the race to earn and accumulate wealth, the English led the way through the 18th and 19th centuries. Great fortunes were made and lost in what would now be called active investment management – or even, dare I say it, hedge funds – as the merchant banks, or investment banks as they are known in the US, and the Stock Exchange whipped up ever more interest in investing – particularly overseas. Trained by the necessity of funding the British government through the Napoleonic Wars, merchant banks such as Barings and Rothschilds became extremely adept and therefore powerful in raising loans for domestic and overseas institutions.

> The volume of overseas loans organized by these merchant banks was enormous. During the 100 years between the end of the Napoleonic Wars and the beginning of the First World War there was a growing stream of foreign issues, some on the London Stock Exchange, some issued directly by the merchant banks to other British banks and investors. In the early 1820s, a number of South American loans were floated, many of them disastrous, and in the late 1830s a succession of US state bonds, several of which also defaulted. Yet despite these early setbacks the trickle of foreign issues swelled to a flood. Between 1880 and 1914 well over £2000 million was invested abroad; in the 1913 peak more than half of all British savings flowed overseas.
>
> *Capital City* by Hamish McRae and Frances Cairncross

The savings that this represented did not tend to be the savings of the ordinary people of Victorian and Edwardian Britain. Then, as now, access to specialist active investment and its superior investment returns – and, in many cases, higher risk – was available only to "those in the know" and those who had the money to join in.

And to hammer home the point that there really is nothing new under the sun in the investment industry at least, 1890 saw the most serious threat to the stability of the City of London with the potential collapse of Barings Bank. The Baring Crisis of 1890 was caused by its heavy investment in South American stocks combined with a sudden and severe withdrawal of credit in the UK.

> With large blocks of temporarily unsaleable loans on its hands, it was unable to meet its immediate liabilities. A crash was avoided, but only by an unprecedented display of co-operation among the City's banks, which the Bank of England bullied into setting up a guarantee fund for Barings of over £17 500 000.
>
> *Capital City* by Hamish McRae and Frances Cairncross

Not as much support was shown for Barings roughly 100 years later when over-extended derivatives trading caused its crash and forced sale to ING for the humiliating sum of £1.

Active investment management has made and lost fortunes for investors for hundreds of years. Hedge funds, in all their guises, are just the most recent incarnation of the work of the trading houses or coffee shops of the past. As with their forebearers, general information on hedge funds can be as difficult to gain access to as it used to be, and the superior investment returns, and sometimes higher risk, are still only available to those in the know. Probably the most famous – and the most reviled, in some quarters – of the hedge fund managers is George Soros. Soros can afford to be cursed by the Prime Minister of Malaysia – who accused him of speculating in the Malaysian ringgit in the summer of 1997. Investors in Soros's Quantum Fund enjoyed compounded net returns of 41% per year between 1990 and 1994.

Hedge funds' very lack of transparency has given rise to their mystique, but their incredible investment returns mean that sophisticated investors need to know more. This book is written to make sure that you enter the arena well-prepared.

HEDGE FUNDS: HISTORY, HYPE AND REALITY

Hedge funds are largely misunderstood. Their very lack of clear definition makes them a difficult investment tool to get to grips with. Six common characteristics which apply to hedge funds are listed here. Modern Portfolio Theory and Post-Modern Portfolio Theory also have their role to play in analyzing hedge funds – and in encouraging traditional fund managers to expand outside of the traditional, long-only investment arena.

The consensus of the hedge fund industry is that the first hedge fund was set up by an American investment manager Alfred W Jones in 1949. The concept of hedging is familiar to all of us – hedging one's bets means attempting to protect oneself from the ravages of the unexpected.

In Jones's case, he wished to avoid market risk on his portfolio of US stocks – so that if the US stockmarkets were to crash suddenly, he would be, in some measure, protected. This also meant that he believed that his stock picking skills could be assessable independently from market movements once his portfolio was protected from a market downturn.

> "A hedge fund is defined by its common characteristics, rather than by one simple definition."

Jones achieved the first "hedging" activities by using shorting techniques combined with gearing or leverage, as it is known in the US. Jones bought what he believed to be undervalued stocks – went long – and sold – shorted – overvalued stocks. In 1952, Jones converted his fund into a multi-manager hedge fund, that is one that invests in a range of other hedge funds under the multi-manager's active management.

A hedge fund is defined by its common characteristics, rather than by one simple definition. From Jones's first hedge fund, we have the two most common characteristics of a hedge fund: a fund that can go long or short and a fund that uses gearing. Beyond that, Jones was reimbursed for his investment expertise through an incentive or performance fee of 20%, a third common characteristic of hedge funds which have performance fees, usually of between 15 and 25%.

Here, we can put paid to one of the greatest myths about hedge funds. Hedge funds are not necessarily "hedged." Jones happened to use long and short techniques to achieve hedging, but many hedge funds don't do that. Many use long and short techniques to arbitrage between different financial instruments or related sectors to profit from price anomalies or expected changes in prices. Confusingly, they would still be classed as hedge funds.

Because hedge funds use a wide variety of specialist investment techniques such as going long, short, or gearing and because many of them employ derivatives, they do not fit the regulations established for investor protection in retail investment funds such as mutual funds in the US or unit trusts in the UK. These regulations are designed to provide a lowest common denominator of investor protection and sophisticated funds aimed at more sophisticated investors do not fit within their framework. Worldwide, investment regulation works on the principle that smaller investors need more protection because they are more likely to be unsophisticated investors who can't afford to lose their savings.

As a result, hedge funds are often based within offshore jurisdictions where investment regulation may be more flexible. If the hedge funds are within the American regulatory framework, they are often within limited partnerships. A fourth common characteristic of hedge funds is that they are based offshore or within limited partnerships in the US.

The minimum investment in hedge funds is often extremely high – US$1m is not unheard of . Many hedge fund managers have a significant part of their net worth in their own fund – indeed a lot of fund of funds managers or hedge fund consultants require this as a sign of good faith – and so the hedge fund arena is full of rich people, both on the investor and investment manager side of the equation.

In this context "rich people" are often euphemistically referred to as "high net worth clients" rather than as institutions which are usually banks or pension or insurance funds. At this level, the divisions between private clients and institutions can become rather blurred. One fund of funds manager refers to his clientele as high net worth clients who are so rich they're practically institutions.

A fund that has a significant investment from its own manager is a fifth common characteristic of hedge funds.

Finally, hedge funds seek to achieve absolute rather than benchmark performance. Traditional investment managers – those who invest pension fund money, for instance – are expected to achieve investment returns which are compared with a benchmark. This benchmark may be an appropriate stock index for the portfolio, such as the S&P 500 for a US equity portfolio or the FT-SE 100 for one in the UK. The traditional manager is deemed to have achieved performance by how closely he manages to mirror his benchmark or the index. This is fine in the last few years of roaring equity markets but when there is a downturn and stock markets go down 25% overnight and the traditional manager follows it, losing 25%, he is in the strange position of having achieved 100% performance for mirroring the benchmark, but has actually lost money. This would not suit the hedge fund manager at all. Hedge fund managers, and other players in the alternative investment arena, prefer to work for absolute returns – not least because if they lose money, they don't get paid their performance fee. If they go up 10%, they have made 10%, if they are down 10%, they have lost 10%.

So, we have six common characteristics of hedge funds by which you may identify the beast when you come across it.

1. Hedge fund managers can go long or short.
2. Hedge fund managers use gearing or leverage.
3. Hedge fund managers are paid through a performance or incentive fee.
4. Hedge funds are often registered offshore.
5. Hedge fund managers often invest their own money in their funds.
6. Hedge fund managers aim for absolute returns.

On the other hand, George Soros, manager of the Quantum Fund and possibly the most famous of the hedge fund managers sums it all up in *The Alchemy of Finance*:

> I started a model portfolio that became a hedge fund (a mutual fund that employs leverage and uses various techniques of hedging) in 1969. I have been in charge of that fund ever since, although I delegated much of the responsibility to others between September 1981 and September 1984. The fund has grown from about $4 million at inception to nearly $2 billion and most of the growth has been internally generated. Origi-

nal investors have seen the value of their shares multiply 300-fold. No investment fund has ever produced comparable results.

More than that, Paul Tudor Jones II, another leading hedge fund manager, estimates that the odds of George Soros compiling the investment record he did as the manager of the Quantum Fund from 1968 through 1993 were 473 million to one.

Nicola Meaden of UK-based hedge and managed futures data suppliers TASS Management sets the following parameters for traditional and alternative investing which further highlight the difference between the two sectors.

Traditional investing – general parameters

- Traditional investing generally takes place in an open and transparent market place.
- The market place is usually highly regulated, implying, but not necessarily delivering plenty of investor protection.
- The market is liquid with lots of buyers and sellers.
- The execution of transactions is speedy.
- The settlement and administrative systems are efficient and transparent.
- There are plenty of brokers/intermediaries allowing participants to shop around for the price and service that they want.
- There are plenty of information sources enabling participants to check or monitor continuously the performance of what they have bought.

Alternative investing – general parameters

- The market place may be neither open nor transparent.
- The market may not be regulated.
- It is often stated that liquidity may be very poor with alternative investments; this is only partly true. Liquidity is usually excellent if you want to buy into something; the problems may arise when you want to get out.

- The settlement and administration systems may be neither transparent nor efficient.
- Information sources are less prevalent making it much more difficult to keep up with what is going on.
- In absolute terms, the fees are usually higher than in the traditional market. On average, an annual management fee of 1.5% and an incentive fee of 20% are charged by the hedge fund.

TECHNICAL TERMS EXPLAINED

In defining hedge funds, I have used a number of terms and concepts that may be new to some readers. Forgive me if I tell you what you already know but it's always useful to cover the basics.

The long and the short of it

Going long undervalued stocks is pretty self-explanatory – the manager buys equities that he thinks are cheap, or perhaps he would prefer to say "good value" at the price, and waits for them to go up, thereby reaping the rewards of capital growth: something that we can all aspire to.

Going short overvalued stocks is a more difficult concept, particularly for private investors in Europe where, until recently, shorting was not a common investment management tool. You have to get your mind around the notion that you can sell something that you haven't got – thereby allowing yourself to profit from market movements in either direction – a premise which lies at the heart of all active investment management techniques.

> "It's always useful to cover the basics."

A fund manager can short stock that he believes will go down in price, by borrowing it from an institution which holds it and selling it. The process, in an extremely simplified version, goes roughly like this.

■ **Example**

Mr Fund Manager decides that Company B is a badly run company in a lousy sector but one which enjoys an over-inflated share price. He approaches his broker and asks him to sell 100 000 shares in Company B. The broker obtains the shares from the Large Building Institution who agrees to lend them. The broker charges Mr Fund Manager an interest rate, known in the US as the Broker Lending Rate, which he continues to charge until the position closes. The institution and Mr Fund Manager are now short 100 000 shares in Company B. The money for the shares is paid by Mr Fund Manager and put on deposit and the broker and the lender take a slice. For its part, the institution now has an income on the 100 000 shares, plus it will have hung on to the dividend of the shares. The shorting process tends to take place in larger capitalization, liquid shares which the institution is very likely to own but is very unlikely to sell, however it is very happy to use them to raise more revenue. Meanwhile, Mr Fund Manager is clearly hoping that the share price of Company B will go down, because he has to cover his position by buying the shares back. Clearly, if the share price goes up, Mr Fund Manager closes at a loss and if it goes down, at a profit.

The two main problems with shorting stock is that it tends to happen only in highly liquid shares and so the flexibility of investing is quite limited. Secondly, the Large Building Institution will have lost its voting rights if it lends out its shares for shorting. If Company B becomes involved in merger and acquisition activity, the institution will want its shares back pronto. This can cause a squeeze on the short sellers which may artificially affect their trading.

A word about derivatives

The other method of going long or shorting stock is through derivatives use but, another myth destroyed, hedge fund managers don't use derivatives as much as people think. A 1996 study by the hedge fund consultants Van Hedge Fund Advisors showed that 24.2% of the sample of different types of funds did not use derivatives, while 46.2% used them for hedging only (see Figure 1.1). A similar study conducted by Van Hedge Fund Advisors in 1995 found that 77% used derivatives not at all or only for hedging. If a fund manager were to use derivatives for going long or short, he would use puts or calls (selling or buying using options) or longs and shorts (using futures).

Fig. 1.1 GLOBAL HEDGE FUNDS USE OF DERIVATIVES AS OF 1996

Hedge fund style	Don't use derivatives	Hedging only	Return enhancements only	Hedging and return enhancement	Total
Aggressive growth	38.7%	39.1%	0.4%	21.8%	61.3%
Distressed securities	41.1%	39.3%	1.8%	17.0%	58.9%
Emerging markets	15.2%	64.0%	0.5%	20.3%	84.8%
Funds of funds	6.4%	47.2%	2.0%	44.5%	93.6%
Income	35.1%	36.5%	0.0%	28.4%	64.9%
Macro	14.1%	25.4%	0.0%	60.6%	85.9%
Market neutral–arbitrage	18.5%	43.8%	1.4%	36.3%	81.5%
Market neutral – securities hedging	32.7%	45.1%	1.0%	21.2%	67.3%
Marketing timing	25.0%	38.2%	7.9%	28.9%	75.0%
Opportunistic	18.8%	37.2%	3.9%	40.1%	81.2%
Several strategies	38.8%	49.0%	0.0%	12.2%	61.2%
Short selling	28.1%	40.6%	0.0%	31.3%	71.9%
Special situations	20.6%	60.3%	0.0%	19.1%	79.4%
Value	32.1%	50.8%	3.2%	13.9%	67.9%
Total sample	**24.2%**	**46.2%**	**1.8%**	**27.8%**	**75.8%**

Source: Van Hedge Fund Advisors

The details need not concern the private investor – the concept is important. This is that active investment managers can sell things they don't own if they think that they are going to go down. Even Soros admits to a "malicious pleasure in making money by selling short stocks that were institutional favorites." (*The Alchemy of Finance*)

Gearing or leverage

The easiest way to describe gearing or leverage is to ask you to think of a small lever heaving a large boulder – or the gears on a car which are designed to make up hill and down dale equally easy for the engine. Gearing is the proverbial double edged sword as the manager is using a small amount of money to make a bigger investment statement. If it goes wrong, it goes wrong in a big way – the small lever breaks and the boulder squashes you, to keep up with the metaphor.

If the manager gets it right, then it can give a huge boost to performance. Soros again:

> Using leverage can produce superior results when the going is good, but it can wipe you out when events fail to conform to your expectations.
>
> *The Alchemy of Finance*

Gearing can be achieved through straightforward borrowing of funds to boost investment in a given strategy or through derivatives. Gearing is implicit in derivatives use because the investor pays only a small part of the price of a derivatives contract at the outset. This is known as margin on futures contracts, or premium on options contract. He then has to pay regular margins or premiums to stay in the game, as it were. This small amount of money is controlling a much larger one. If the investor gets it wrong and the market moves in a different direction from that which he had expected, he will have to pay in full at the expiration of the contract and may have lost a considerably larger amount of money than he can afford or made a considerably larger amount of money than he would have expected.

Net long positions

Hedge fund managers often refer to the status of their funds in terms of a "net long position." This is a term which attempts to encompass the actual position of the portfolio with its longs, shorts and gearing taken into consideration. George P Van of Van Hedge Fund Advisors, writing in *Pension Management* in August 1995, described measuring hedging in the following way.

> How does a hedge fund manager measure the extent of hedging? A "typical" hedge fund manager with $100 in capital might choose to use leverage to buy shares valued at $120, and to sell short shares valued at $60. His or her gross investment therefore is $180 ($120 plus $60) or 180% of the investors' capital. However, the net exposure is only $60 ($120 long minus $60 short). The portfolio is biased toward long expo-

sure, so it is described as 60% net long ($60 "net exposure" divided by $100 capital).

SOME INVESTMENT THEORIES ...

Before we start to look at specific hedge fund investment sectors, it will be useful to have a little background on investment and modern investment theories.

In the beginning investment was very easy – you either owned something or you didn't. Then, as we heard earlier, the growth of trade forced new concerns to raise their heads. The value of the thing that you owned might be at risk from natural disasters, competition or a

> "The concept of protecting things from risk lies at the heart of the development of the derivatives markets."

change in sentiment. The addition of risk to the equation meant that you had to protect what you owned, which cost money, which meant that you had to earn more and so it went on.

Suddenly, in the late 18th and in the 19th century, manufacturing companies had shares which were subject to the vagaries of a stock market where sentiment, which often had nothing at all to do with the commercial success of these companies, could decide their value on a day-by-day basis.

Origin of futures

The concept of protecting things from risk lies at the heart of the development of the derivatives markets.

> ... the modern origins of futures, certainly as an exchange-based industry, lie in the productive fields of the grain belt in the US in the first half of the last century and the cruel exigencies of supply and demand. Price fluctuations for grain were violently volatile which had a serious and noticeable effect on the economy by causing an increase in the price of food. At harvest time in the last century, the prairie-based farmer hauled his wagon load of grain to Chicago, and once there hunted for a buyer – along with every other farmer who had hauled his wagon load

of grain to Chicago. In the way of these things, the price went firmly down as the farmer was forced to accept whatever was offered for his crop – or worse as he was forced to watch it spoil and be dumped in Lake Michigan. Come the late spring and early summer, harvest stocks were used up, available grain was in great demand and short supply and the wise grain merchant who still had supplies made a lot of money – while everybody else suffered.

Managed Futures – An Investor's Guide by Beverly Chandler

The solution was found in the establishment of the Chicago Board of Trade, to this day, the biggest of the futures exchanges. Here, a farmer could protect the value of his crop by agreeing a price while it still sat in the field.

Traditional fund management

Meanwhile, the 19th century saw a rapid growth in pension and insurance funds managed by professional fund managers. Indeed, the US concept of "the prudent man rule" dates from 1830 in a statement made by Judge Samuel Putnam on a case which questioned the investment management of an estate by its trustees. Peter Bernstein tells the story in *Against the Gods*:

In rendering his decision in the case, Justice Samuel Putnam concluded that the trustees had conducted themselves "honestly and discreetly and carefully, according to the existing circumstances in the discharge of their trusts". He declared that trustees cannot be held accountable for a loss of capital that was not owing to their wilful default. "... If that were otherwise, who would undertake such hazardous responsibility?" He continued with what came to be immortalized as the Prudent Man Rule:

"Do what you will, the capital is at hazard ... All that can be required of a trustee to invest is, that he shall conduct himself faithfully and exercise a sound discretion. He is to observe how men of prudence, discretion and intelligence manage their own affairs, not in regard to speculation, but in regard to the permanent disposition of their funds, considering the probable income, as well as the probable safety of the capital to be invested."

And so traditional investment management from that date onwards was dominated by the Prudent Man Rule.

In 1952 an American academic journal, the *Journal of Finance*, published an extensive piece by a 25 year old graduate student who was studying under Milton Friedman; Friedman won the Nobel prize for his work on monetary economics at the University of Chicago. At the time Friedman dismissed the work with: "This is not economics." From a relatively low-key start, came a seminal work. Harry Markowitz's "portfolio selection" was the first step on the road to the modern approach to investment management, and indeed Markowitz's work (which came to be known as modern portfolio theory) earned him a Nobel prize in Economic Science in 1990.

Modern portfolio theory

(with thanks to Richard Johnson of Barra International Ltd, London)

Within his 1952 paper, Markowitz demonstrated that a portfolio is a sum of its parts and should be assessed in its entirety, rather than holding by holding. He believed that diversification, and the cutting of risk that this offered, could only be achieved if each part of a portfolio worked differently from the others. This was pretty revolutionary stuff in the early 1950s when investments went up or down and the notion of constructing a portfolio that spread that volatility across all types of market sectors and conditions was totally unheard of.

In 1959, Markowitz followed up his original paper with "Portfolio selection: efficient diversification of investments." Here he outlined a methodology which allowed the fund manager to find the most efficient portfolio for his purposes.

> His work then turned to demonstrating that portfolios have theoretical levels of efficiency or natural points of balance. For any particular level of risk, he showed that there is a point where the yield could be optimized. These theories produced what later became known as the portfolio's efficient frontier. Once the investor's preferences as a rational being have been quantified and slotted into a mathematical model, it is a simple step from that to identify the investor's optimal portfolios, as a point along the line that constitutes the efficient frontier.
>
> *Managed Futures – An Investor's Guide* by Beverly Chandler

Risk is the underlying concept in modern portfolio theory and at least some basic explanation of risk is necessary to understand it. Risk is usually defined as the variability of returns. This can best be illustrated using a simple example.

■ Risk – an example

Stock A

Month	1	2	3	4	5	6
Return	2%	4%	−1%	3.5%	2.5%	1%

The table above shows Stock A's return over 6 months (in 1 its price increased 2% ... etc.). Its average (or *mean*) monthly return over the period is the total return divided by the number of months: $[2 + 4 + (-1) + 3.5 + 2.5 + 1]/6 = 2\%$.

We use this mean to calculate the variability of returns (or *variance*). First we subtract the mean from each month's return. Below we will represent the percentages as decimals (2% = 0.02, 2 out of 100):

Stock A

Month	1	2	3	4	5	6
Return	0.02	0.04	−0.01	0.035	0.025	0.01
Return – Mean	0	0.02	−0.03	0.015	0.005	−0.01

Next we square the de-meaned returns:

Stock A

Month	1	2	3	4	5	6
Return	0.02	0.04	−0.01	0.035	0.025	0.01
Return – Mean	0	0.02	−0.03	0.015	0.005	−0.01
(Return – Mean)^2	0	0.0004	0.0009	0.000225	0.000025	0.0001

This makes all the resulting numbers positive and puts more emphasis on the larger deviations. And then add the resulting numbers together to get 0.00165. And then divide by $N - 1$ (where N is the number of months) to get 0.00033. This is the stock's variance.

Now let's say we have another stock whose monthly returns are shown below:

Stock B

Month	1	2	3	4	5	6
Return	6%	5%	−1.5%	4.5%	7.5%	−0.5%

We can calculate this stock's mean to be 3.5 and variance 0.00133. Stock A and Stock B can be plotted on a graph as shown in Figure 1.2.

Fig. 1.2 RISK-RETURN GRAPH 1

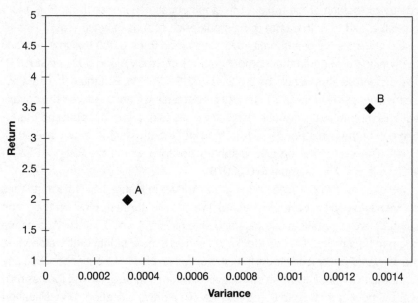

Figure 1.2 clearly shows how stock B has higher return than stock A but higher risk also.

Fig. 1.3 RISK-RETURN GRAPH 2

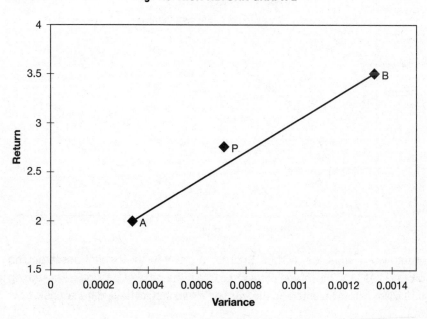

Another concept in MPT is *covariance*. We can see that stocks A and B covary by looking at the table. Both stock prices rise in months 1, 2, 4 and 5 but fall in period 3. In month 6 the stock price of A rises while that of B falls. Using statistics we can quantify this covariance to be 0.00045. Now let's say that we had a portfolio that comprised 50% of Stock A and 50% of Stock B. The expected return would be 0.5*2 + 0.5*3.5 = 2.75%. But the risk would *not* be the sum of the individual risks. This is because we have ignored the covariance term. Intuitively, we can think of this as taking into account the offsetting risk of the two stocks – e.g., in the sixth month stock A rose while stock B fell. The risk of the equally weighted portfolio would be $Risk_A$ + $Risk_B$ – 2*Covariance. This is equal to 0.00076.

We can plot this portfolio on the graph shown in Figure 1.3. Note that P lies above a straight line between A and B. We can plot further points on the graph using different combinations of A and B (e.g. 25%A and 75% B). And as we begin to hold more than two stocks we can plot more points until we arrive at the *efficient frontier* (see Figure 1.4). It is called an efficient frontier because any point within it is inefficient – a same level of return can be achieved for less risk, e.g. by moving from P_1 to P_2 – this is known as diversification. Diversification enables an investor to reduce his risk without reducing return.

Fig. 1.4 RISK-RETURN GRAPH 3

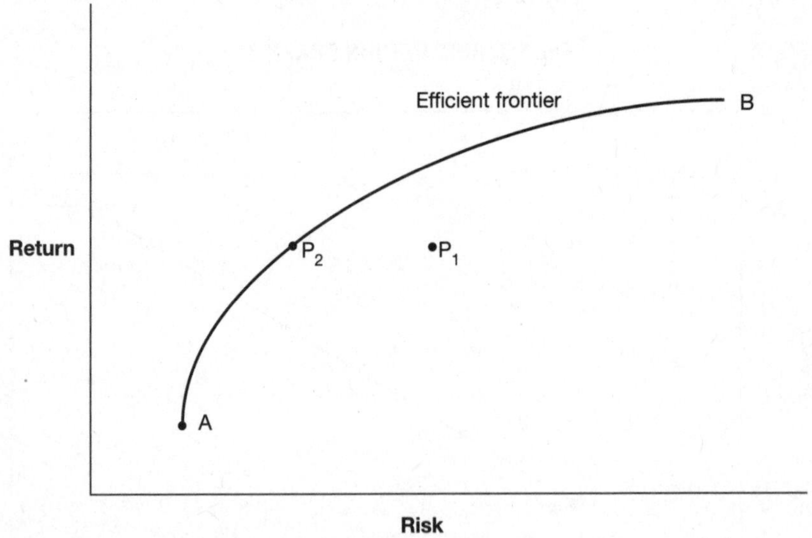

Markowitz's work led William Sharpe to develop the capital asset pricing model (CAPM). This model aimed to explain the price of securities, assuming that all investors invested on the frontier. If two stocks have different risk, how will their prices differ in terms of how much an investor is willing to pay for them, given that he wants to be on the efficient frontier? (The CAPM usually takes up about two chapters in books on investment theory!) The CAPM was followed by another model known as APT (arbitrage pricing theory) and MPT itself has now been succeeded by Post-Modern Portfolio Theory which is designed to cover the increasing use of non-linear derivative securities and the more complicated over-the-counter (OTC) derivatives tailored specifically to suit a client's requirements, e.g., a manager may want to hedge risk arising from exposure to French oil companies), and the rise of hedge funds, like George Soros's which bet against the pound by short-selling sterling on Black Wednesday. These offer high levels of return due to their leveraged nature.

Tracking error

Instead of looking at a portfolio's total risk, analysts often prefer to look at its risk relative to a benchmark. In the UK this is often the FTSE-100 index, although there are many others (FT250, Small Cap...). The variability of a portfolio's return relative to a benchmark is known as "tracking error" (or sometimes "active risk"). Investment managers will typically want to out-perform the benchmark while keeping risk at a reasonable level. The level of risk a manager is prepared to accept for a given level of return depends on his individual "risk aversion."

Fig. 1.5 RISK-RETURN GRAPH 4

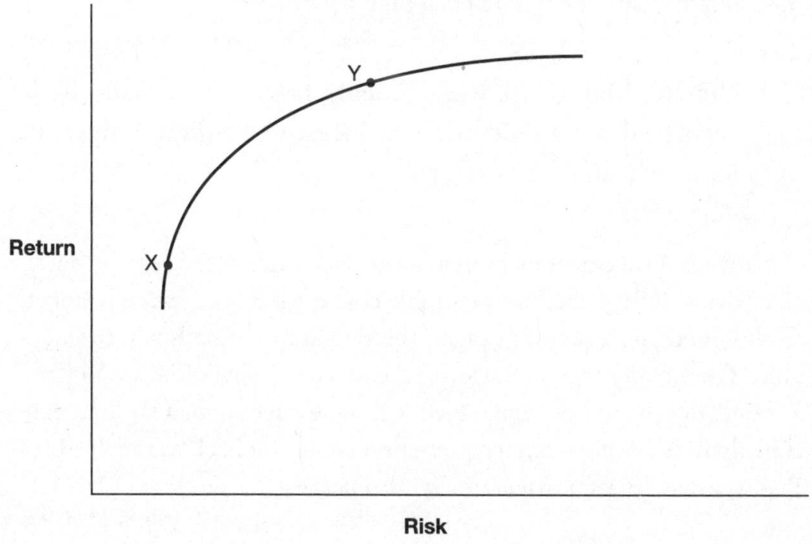

17

A risk averse investor would prefer X, but a less risk averse investor would prefer Y (see Figure 1.5). Both portfolios are efficient.

The stock basket tracking error graph is a graph of optimized portfolios with a constrained number of stocks, i.e., they are all on the efficient frontier, given the number of maximum number of stocks allowed. Thus it shows the minimum tracking error possible for a given number of stocks. What one can conclude is that with a sophisticated optimization algorithm (such computer packages are a day-to-day part of modern investing), risk can be diversified away to a satisfactory level with just 30-odd stocks. Obviously with 100 stocks tracking error is zero as we will simply hold the index.

When risk next reared its head and threatened reward, investment managers took the original lesson of Markowitz to their hearts. Bernstein again:

> Then, in the late 1960s, the aggressive, performance-oriented managers of mutual fund portfolios began to be regarded as folk heroes, people like Gerry Tsai of the Manhattan Fund ("What is the Chinaman doing?" was a popular question along Wall Street) and John Hartwell of the Hartwell & Campbell Growth Fund ("[Performance means] seeking to get better than average results over a fairly long period of time – consistently"). It took the crash of 1973–4 to convince investors that these miracle-workers were just high rollers in a bull market and that they too should be interested in risk as well as return. While the Standard & Poor's 500 fell by 43% from December 1972 to September 1974, the Manhattan Fund lost 60% and the Hartwell & Campbell fund fell by 55%.
>
> Peter L Bernstein, *Against the Gods*

In this climate, Markowitz was suddenly fashionable. What he had actually achieved was to identify that investors could use diversification to limit the variance of return.

Bernstein again:

> Variance is a statistical measurement of how widely the returns on an asset swing around their average. The concept is mathematically linked to the standard deviation; in fact, the two are essentially interchangeable. The greater the variance or the standard deviation around the average, the less the average return will signify about what the outcome is likely to be. A high-variance situation lands you back in the head-in-the-oven-feet-in-the-refrigerator syndrome.
>
> Peter L Bernstein, *Against the Gods*

While modern portfolio theory and post modern portfolio theory are worthy of, and indeed have been served by, many books and theses in their own right, for the purposes of this book, the most important contribution of modern portfolio theory is that it allowed institutional managers to consider diversification out of the traditional investment arena, and gave marketing managers for non-traditional – and therefore non-correlating – investment funds something to talk about.

> "The most important contribution of modern portfolio theory is that it allowed institutional managers to consider diversification out of the traditional investment arena."

Most investors, whether institutional or private, want returns but few want them with very high volatility. If diversification into an investment fund based on chicken-entrail divining demonstrably cut the volatility of return on a portfolio, then investors would want to know about it. It is this premise that lies behind the development of the whole active investment management industry.

Active investment management

Active investment management has become something of a catch-all name for investment managers who work in the hedge fund, currency fund and managed futures fund industries. However, traditional fund managers also use the term, implying active investment management – investing in long-only equities or bonds – rather than indexation, whereby they invest in the indices of relevant markets and seek to achieve returns as close to the index as possible.

Managed futures

Managed futures fund managers, known as commodity trading advisors (CTAs), invest in exchange-traded futures and options of all types, often using a computer-based trading system. Because of the wide variety of markets that they trade, their returns are often negatively correlated with any other type of investment management. Philip L Yang, Jr and Richard G Faux, Jr of Willowbridge Associates Inc, write in *Evaluating and Implementing Hedge Fund Strategies*, edited by Ronald A Lake:

Managed futures and hedge funds have interacted in a variety of ways over the years. Some of the best-known hedge fund managers, Bruce Kovner, Paul Tudor Jones and Louis Bacon, for example, began as managed futures experts. Their participation in common stocks (and other specialized cash market trading techniques more typical of hedge fund managers) only occurred as the size of assets under their management increased. At the same time, well-known hedge fund managers, such as George Soros, Julian Robertson and Michael Steinhardt, who began with an emphasis on equity market investing, diversified as their assets expanded into markets normally associated with managed futures (currency, financial and commodity futures). This convergence of techniques has tended to blur the differences between managed futures and hedge fund trading techniques ... there are a number of factors that caused this convergence of techniques to occur. The most important are:

- the liquidity and diversity of the futures markets
- the opportunity to profit in declining as well as rising markets, and
- the generally low correlation between managed futures' trading results and the performance of traditional fixed income, equity and other hedge fund investments.

Two of the leading suppliers of data for the hedge fund industry, Managed Account Reports in New York, and TASS Management in the UK, started with the managed futures industry and have expanded into the hedge fund industry. The European Managed Futures Association has also expanded out of the managed futures arena with a name change to the Alternative Investment Management Association.

While many would put the two sectors in together, I feel that they are different beasts. Rightly or wrongly, investors have not always received the notion of managed futures funds with unalloyed delight because of the use of the word "futures" in the name, conjuring up images of wild derivatives trading and cataclysmic financial disaster. As an act of casuistry, some managed futures funds, which are quite clearly futures funds, have re-named themselves or quietly slipped over into the hedge fund sector. There is nothing wrong with any of this but, if size is an indication of preference, then hedge funds are considerably more popular with investors than managed futures, as we shall see in the next chapter.

THE HEDGE FUND UNIVERSE: SIZE AND STRUCTURE

Along with the lack of a simple definition of hedge funds, no consensus exists on the size of the industry. Funds also come in a variety of structures and there are funds of funds which offer access to other hedge funds. None of these structures come for free and there is a constant debate about fees in the hedge fund industry.

Rather like the problem of definition within the industry, estimates on the amount of money under management in this investment sector vary considerably. The New York-based hedge fund data collectors MAR/Hedge has 1100 hedge funds in its database, representing $92.2 billion in assets. Global macro managers account for 42.2% of the total, down from 53.7% in 1996. Global managers are now the second largest category with 27.5% of the assets (see Figures 2.1 and 2.2).

Fig. 2.1 ASSETS IN EACH STYLE 1997

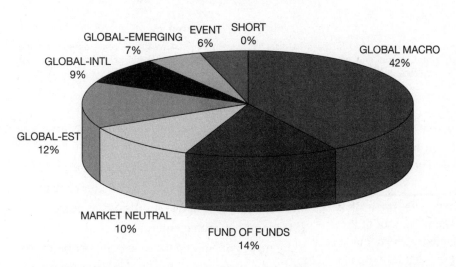

Of the $92.9 billion represented in the MAR/Hedge database, global macro managers account for 42.2% of the total, down from 53.7% in 1996. Global managers are the second largest category, with 27.5% of the assets; almost half is in the established markets sub-category.

Source: MAR/Hedge, Managed Account Reports Inc

Tennesse-based Van Hedge Fund Advisors believes that the overall universe is 4100 funds with unleveraged assets of $236bn.

TASS Management estimates the size of the industry at end September 1997 at $150bn of which at least 80% of all managers are

Fig. 2.2 AVERAGE ASSETS BY STYLE 1997

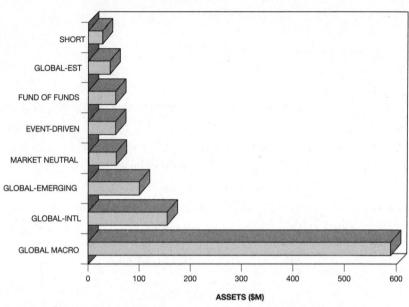

ASSETS ($M)

The average fund in the database has assets of $104 million. Global macro, and the international and emerging markets sub-categories of the global style, have the largest average amount of assets under management.

Source: MAR/Hedge, Managed Account Reports Inc

based in the US with the UK having the second largest concentration of hedge fund managers.

Richard Hills, writing in *Hedge Funds – An Introduction to Skill-Based Investment Strategies*, estimates that there are nearly 5000 hedge funds with more than $300bn under management.

> **"Whatever the truth is about the size of the industry, most would agree that it is big and growing"**

By now, you can begin to see the problem. As Philipp Cottier explains in *Hedge Funds and Managed Futures*:

Figures with respect to the size of the hedge fund industry are difficult to obtain. Estimates for the end of 1995 range from 1300 funds managing $80bn to 4000 funds managing $250bn. The real number must lie somewhere between these two extremes. The largest 34 hedge funds (each managing over $500m) already exceed $57bn. Any attempt at an estimate encounters the problems of inadequate data and inconsistent definitions.

Figure 2.3 shows the figures for funds under management by hedge funds and managed hedge fund accounts.

Whatever the truth is about the size of the industry, most would agree that it is big and growing. MAR/Hedge's research shows that only 10% of the funds in its database have a track record of over 10 years, while 71% have a less than five year track record.

The reasons why it is difficult to account for the size of the industry is because of the lack of a clear definition – what some may include, others wouldn't – and because the work of fund of funds managers may cause double accounting, or may take a significant fund of funds out of the market place by creating it for one family or an institutional investor.

Fig. 2.3 HEDGE FUNDS AND MANAGED HEDGE FUND ACCOUNTS: FUNDS UNDER MANAGEMENT (IN MILLIONS USD, END OF 1995)

Category	Number of funds	Total assets under mgt.	US funds and accounts	Non-US funds and accounts
Single manager hedge funds (excluding multi-manager funds and feeder funds)	2,500	170,000	80,000	90,000
Managed hedge fund accounts (single manager accounts only)	n/a	30,000	20,000	10,000
Multi-manager hedge funds	500	50,000	20,000	30,000
Total hedge fund industry (excluding double counting caused by multi-manager and feeder structures)	n/a	200,000	100,000	100,000

Source: Hedge Funds and Managed Futures by Dr Philipp Cottier

FUND STRUCTURES

The breadth of the investment arena in which hedge funds operate is so broad that they often don't fit into standard investment fund structures which are limited in the scope of their investments. This means that they are often incorporated offshore and are unlikely to be publicly available – they can't advertise in the press or distribute marketing material to private individuals. There will be more detail on the legal issues surrounding hedge funds in Chapter 7 but here is a simple guide to the most commonly used hedge fund structures.

Open-ended and closed-ended funds

An open-ended fund is one in which shares are continuously issued and redeemed. A closed-ended structure is one that has a fixed capital status which, after an initial subscription period when all the shares may have been taken up, is then closed to new investment. Shares of the closed-ended structure can be traded on a secondary market by a market maker or on a stock exchange. This can provide a very useful way into hedge funds for investors who don't want to commit the full minimum investment in a hedge fund – often $1m. However, a secondary market in shares of a successful hedge fund can often run at a premium to the true price of the shares, or at a discount. The investor is taking on another level of risk when investing in hedge funds in this manner.

A company structure

Investors may buy shares in a company whose business is to be a hedge fund – the UK investment trust has this structure. Company ownership may bring with it normal shareholder requirements such as voting on various issues, attending shareholder meetings and defending against or being part of merger and acquisition activity. A company listing on a stock exchange for a hedge fund may make it available as an investment tool to institutions who are prohibited from investing in unregulated funds. This is particularly common in Europe, where many funds have chosen to be listed on an offshore exchange such as Luxembourg or Dublin.

Trusts

Trusts are the oldest of the investment industry structures. The investor puts his money into a trust which then owns it. The trust is then run by its trustee, advised by the beneficiary. Giving your assets to a trust has proved to be an extremely tax-efficient and flexible method of investing for a number of people over the years.

Collective investment schemes

These are largely aimed at smaller, retail investors. They are known as unit trusts in the UK, mutual funds in the US and ucits (the undertaking for collective investments in transferable securities) in the newly "merged" EU. The concept is simple – each investor's small amount of savings is mixed with others to create a large pool that can invest in the markets. There are no hedge funds structured in this way because the costs and coming and going of investment capital (as small investors invest and redeem) would make the product untenable.

The closest that the UK has come to producing an actively managed investment product aimed at the general retail market lies within the unit trust universe. This is the futures and options fund (the Fof) and the geared futures and options fund (the Gfof).

Ucits were developed to allow passporting of investment funds across international borders within the EU. As with most products designed by a committee, the investment limitations placed upon ucits have made them unsuitable for use by the hedge fund industry at this time.

Partnerships

The US private placement partnership is the most common structure for US investors. They are limited to 99 investors, at least 65 of whom must be accredited. Within a partnership structure, the partners own the assets and they are not transferable without the consent of the other partners. In general partnerships, partners share the liability while in limited liability partnerships, one general partner (often the fund's manager) has the unlimited liability, while the remaining partners have limited liability.

Managed accounts

These are a more flexible structure than the fund structure to establish, but equally they lack the security of a fund. They are literally an account managed by a money manager on a discretionary basis for the investor. The account is usually held at a custodian bank and the trading is executed and cleared through an independent broker whose statements are sent to the client so that he can keep up with what is happening with his investment.

Prime brokers

Prime brokers are used by hedge fund managers to organize their back office and administrative activities.

Originally, a prime broker acted as a recorder of transactions, long and short, but now a prime broker will offer a wide range of services. Richard Harriton of Bear, Stearns Securitites Corp explains in *Evaluating and Implementing Hedge Fund Strategies* that a prime broker will offer services including:

- global custody
- international trade clearing
- creative financing
- customized portfolio reporting
- global securities lending.

Figure 2.4 illustrates the role of the prime broker in the fund management process.

Fig. 2.4 THE ROLE OF THE PRIME BROKER IN THE FUND MANAGEMENT PROCESS

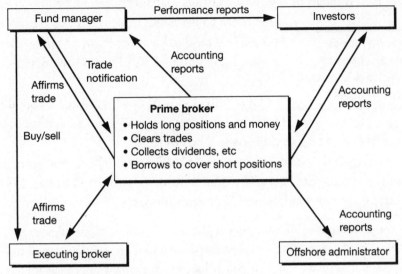

Source: *Evaluating and Implementing Hedge Fund Strategies*, edited by Ron Lake

Funds of funds or multi-manager funds

These are funds which invest in other funds or managed accounts. The advantages that this structure can offer the private investor include the fact that a professional manager, often known as a consultant, makes the investment decision of which funds to invest in for you. The investment decisions are usually based on extensive research undertaken by the fund of funds managers and because one fund of funds manager or consultant may represent a larger "collective investment" in one hedge fund he is likely to have more weight behind him when dealing with hedge fund managers – the good old "pooling" power used within the mutual fund industry.

A significant advantage for private investors who use fund of funds managers lies in the fact that the minimum investment is likely to be lower than that required by individual hedge funds. Currently, there is speculation that a particularly successful hedge fund manager may re-open his fund for investment, with a $10m minimum investment level.

Beyond that, a fund of funds manager may gain access to hedge funds that are closed or have been closed for a number of years.

However, investors in funds of funds are paying the hedge fund's fees plus the fees of the fund of funds manager so it can be an expensive route to investing in hedge funds. Funds of funds' fees tend to be at the least, a management fee of 1.25% up to 2%, plus a performance fee of between 0% and 10%.

> "Generally, funds of funds are used by smaller private investors or institutions."

Generally, funds of funds are used by smaller private investors or institutions. Larger customers may establish their own funds of funds.

Writing in the third *International Hedge Fund Report*, published by fund of funds managers The Momentum Group, in October 1996, Marty Gross of Sandalwood Securities Inc says:

Funds of funds are not simply unbalanced conglomerations of managers but employ increasingly sophisticated techniques to create balance and reduce risk. Each fund of funds has an investment approach that is determined by the strategies of the underlying hedge funds to which it allocates its capital. In deciding whether to invest in a fund of funds, investors must understand these investment characteristics. There are two basic questions investors should ask:

1. What is the investment approach of the fund of funds manager?
2. How does he or she intend to implement it?

There are four basic options available to the fund of funds manager:

1. Target return – the fund of funds manager allocates capital to hedge funds in an attempt to generate a target return usually in the 10 to 15% range. Many fund of funds managers with this goal have used various market neutral strategies along with lower risk distressed securities strategies.
2. Maximum return approach – fund of funds managers select those hedge funds whose investment strategies they believe generate the highest return under current market conditions and are willing to accept a greater volatility as a result.
3. Dedicated strategy – in a dedicated strategy fund, the fund of funds manager selects hedge funds that invest in a particular asset class such as emerging markets, or in event driven strategies such as distressed securities and merger arbitrage.
4. Combinations of the above – under this option the fund of funds

manager mixes lower risk strategies with more aggressive ones to create a fund with a more balanced risk profile.

Gross also prepared a chart which showed a hypothetical example of the effect of allocating capital among four diverse and significantly uncorrelated strategies, each having compound annual returns of 20% and standard deviations in the mid-teens.

Conflicts of interest, rebating fees and soft dollars

Investors need to be aware that there is a potential conflict of interest for fund of funds managers or consultants who offer funds of funds and also represent hedge funds. Many fund of funds managers accept rebated fees from managers they represent as clients. Investors investing with consultants are at perfect liberty to ask what percentage – if any – of the consultant's revenue comes from rebates and what happens to the rebates – are they put back into the fund or kept by the fund of funds managers? It is generally an emerging hedge fund manager with between $60m and $100m who is quite likely to rebate part of his fee to a fund of funds manager.

Soft dollars

Soft dollars are private arrangements which enable the brokerage fees of a fund to be refunded to the fund of funds manager in the form of a research tool, such as a database system or a subscription to an online information provider such as Bloombergs, or some other project. Again, the investor need have no fear of asking a fund of funds manager if he is getting soft dollar commissions from funds. Indeed, most reputable firms disclose such a practice in their prospectuses – look under "fees and expenses."

Writing in *MAR/Hedge*, in February 1997, Lois Peltz recommends the investor to be cautious about a consultant who works for a brokerage firm or has a brokerage firm affiliation.

Guaranteed funds

Guaranteed fund structures were invented by the managed futures industry and proved to be one of the most useful marketing tools for spreading the managed futures sector among retail clients. The idea is simple, the fund's capital is split, perhaps into 60/40 or 75/25 and the larger part is invested in a high-grade security such as zero coupon bonds, and the smaller part in the "risky" investment. The fund investment has a lifespan dictated by the expiration date of the guaranteed part. By the end of the lifespan, often five or seven years, the zero coupon bond will have matured, guaranteeing that the investor gets his original capital back, while the other part of the portfolio, in an ideal world, offers the cream on the cake, with an investment return which far outweighs that of other investment vehicles.

Guaranteed funds or other structured products are not yet common in the hedge fund world because they are based on the premise that investors are likely to, or are worried about, losing their money. Unlike managed futures, the losses shown by hedge fund managers tend to be less extreme – good hedge fund managers iron out and thus avoid volatility. While guaranteed funds do have their place for the private investor, they are costly to run – because of their complicated structure – and effectively offer the investor access to a geared bond fund. As hedge funds grow in popularity and become better known as investment vehicles, we may see versions that are more aimed at the retail market where concern of loss of capital may be greater, and these may include a guarantee structure.

FEES

Fees on hedge funds come in two forms: the performance fee and the management fee. The most common rates are between 1 and 1.5% for the management fee and 20–25% for the performance fee. The former fee is designed to cover the management costs of the hedge fund but it is the latter fee, the performance fee, which has raised some eyebrows among the investor community.

A hedge fund's performance or incentive fee is either charged on a net new high basis, estimated over a given timeframe, or on a hurdled basis where in order to get paid the fund manager has to beat a pre-set hurdle – maybe set at 300 to 500 basis points over dollar libor, for a UK fund, or a rate equal to the amount that would have been earned by investing in 90 day US Treasury Bills for a US fund. If you believe that you are investing with the best by going into hedge funds, then you will expect to pay for it. And payment based on performance is a pretty confident way of charging for services.

Many hedge fund managers are wealthy in their own right (30 hedge fund people were on *Financial World's* list of top paid Wall Streeters in 1995 according to *MAR/Hedge*) and could easily give up investing other people's money and concentrate on their own. But in my many interviews with hedge fund managers, they often say that they wouldn't trust anyone else to invest their money and if they are trading for themselves, they may as well trade for others. For many hedge fund managers, managing money is not a job, it's a way of life.

> "If you believe that you are investing with the best by going into hedge funds, then you will expect to pay for it."

There are a few twists to watch out for in looking at fees. Emerging hedge fund managers often offer a special arrangement on fees, charging only the performance fee and no management fee at the outset of their trading. This could be a good way in for an investor – if the fund manager emerges as very good.

Check what period the net new highs are registered over – obviously the shorter the timespans, maybe monthly, the more performance fees will be paid. Beware of funds that close to new investment and then re-open with a new "new high" to beat. Find out whether the performance fee will be based on total gains or only those that beat a hurdle or benchmark and also see whether there is a high water mark – do funds have to recoup from past losses before the performance fee is activated again? Also watch out for redemption fees – these are more common in structured products which would actually bear a cost if an investor comes out early. However, one does see them with regular hedge funds. Finally look at the fund's policy for redemptions – there may be a lengthy restriction on withdrawal of funds, maybe a 12 month notice period?

I will be incorporating these tips into the Hedge Funds Risk Measurer in Chapter 5 (see pages 131–3).

HEDGE FUND INVESTMENT: SECTORS AND STYLES

Hedge funds have no clear set of investment sectors. Hedge fund managers invest in all sorts of different things – with a definition which is so broad, other types of funds have crept into the hedge fund arena. Here are the most common of the hedge fund styles.

A natural companion to the difficulty in achieving a clear definition of a hedge fund is the fact that there is no clear set of investment sectors in which they invest. Not only can I not simply tell you what a hedge fund is, I also can't simply tell you what it invests in. But don't give up. The problem is that the sector has become so broad that more and more types of funds are included in hedge fund databases which were formerly quite happy in standard investment databases – emerging market funds, for instance. And of course no-one told the hedge fund managers that they had to stick in their appropriate niches and so many hedge funds do a bit of everything.

The style definitions shown in Figure 3.1 come from *MAR/Hedge* and cover pretty much all types of hedge funds on offer at the moment.

From that list, I intend to focus on the following sectors which cover the bulk of the hedge funds on offer:

- global macro
- global international
  - established
  - emerging
- event driven
  - risk arbitrage
  - distressed securities
- market neutral
  - long/short
  - convertible arbitrage
  - bond arbitrage
  - mortgage backed securities
- short sellers.

In Chapter 6 you will find interviews with hedge fund managers who operate in some of these sectors.

Fig. 3.1 HEDGE FUND STYLE DEFINITIONS

Type	Sub-type	Description
Event driven	• Risk arbitrage	Investment theme is dominated by events that are seen as special situations or opportunities to capitalize from price fluctuations.
		Manager simultaneously buys stock in a company being acquired and sells stock in its acquirers. If the takeover falls through, traders can be left with large losses.
	• Distressed securities	Focus is on the securities of companies that are in bankruptcy, reorganization or other corporate restructuring.
Funds of funds	• Diversified	Capital is allocated among funds, providing investors with access to managers with higher minimums than an individual might afford.
		Allocates capital to a variety of fund types
	• Niche	Allocates capital to a specific type of fund
Global	• International	Manager pays attention to economic change around the world (except US) but more bottom-up oriented in that they tend to be stock-pickers in markets they like. Use index derivatives to a much lesser extent than macro managers.
	• Regional – established	Focuses on opportunities in established markets. US opportunity, European opportunity and Japanese opportunity.
	• Regional – emerging	Manager invests in less mature financial markets of the world. Because shorting is not permitted in many emerging markets, managers must go to cash or other markets when valuations make being long unattractive. Focuses on specific regions of the world.

Asia   Hong Kong   Pacific Rim
Australia   India   Pakistan
China   Latin America   Russia
Eastern Europe   Middle East   Singapore

Global macro	• Opportunistic	Manager profits from changes in global economies, typically based on major interest rate shifts, uses leverage and derivatives.
Long only/leveraged		Traditionally equity funds structured like hedge funds; use leverage and incentive fee.
Market neutral	• Long/short	Manager attempts to lock-out or neutralize market risk. In theory, market risk is greatly reduced but it is difficult to make a profit on a large diversified portfolio, so stock-picking is critical
	• Arbitrage – convertible	Net exposure to market risk is believed to be reduced by having equal allocations on the long and short sides of the market. One of the more conservative styles. Manager goes long convertible securities and short underlying equities, profiting from mispricing in the relationship of the two.
	• Arbitrage – stocks	Manager buys a basket of stocks and sells short stock index futures contract, or reverse.
	• Arbitrage – bonds	Manager buys T-bonds and sells short other T-bonds that replicate the bond purchased in terms of rate and maturity.
Sector	• Industry focus	Invests in companies in sectors of the economy Health care Oil and gas Financial services Real estate Food and beverage Technology Media and communications Transportation Natural resources Utilities
Short sellers		Manager takes a position that stock prices will go down. A hedge fund borrows stock and sells it, hoping to buy it back at a lower price. Manager shorts only overvalued securities. A hedge for long-only portfolios and those who feel market is approaching a bearish trend.

Source: MAR/Hedge

GLOBAL MACRO HEDGE FUNDS

These are the largest of the hedge funds and are likely to be the ones that you heard about in the press which first attracted you to the sector. Traditionally, global macro hedge funds have been the largest in terms of money under management but research published in *MAR/Hedge* October 1997 (see Figure 3.2) shows that other investment styles are creeping up on them. The MAR database tracks 14 managers who have at least $1bn in assets under management – a total pool of $44.1bn. There are now more market neutral managers among the larger funds and event-driven, global established and global emerging are gaining in numbers as well. But in terms of assets, macro is still king and the most famous of the global macro hedge fund managers is, undoubtedly, George Soros, and his Quantum Fund is likewise the most famous of the global macro funds.

> "A simple understanding of these types of funds can be reached if you just concentrate on the word 'macro.'"

Fig. 3.2 COMPARING ASSET GROWTH BY STYLE

	Assets Aug 97	Assets Aug 96	Number of funds Aug 97	Number of funds Aug 96
Event driven	$5.6bn	$3.3bn	95	50
Market neutral	9.1	5.7	148	101
Global: Regional estab.	11.3	8.3	235	228
Global: Regional emerg.	6.2	4.0	58	58
Global: International	7.9	6.3	55	47
Global macro	38.9	37.8	67	51
Short sellers	0.3	0.2	8	6
Fund of funds	12.8	10.2	220	164

Source: MAR/Hedge

A simple understanding of these types of funds can be reached if you just concentrate on the word "macro." Macro fund managers look at the big picture, assessing opportunities and risks in the global market place. The global macro fund manager can invest anywhere and in anything, seeking out the opportunity to benefit from an economic imbalance in any corner of the world. Soros describes it as positioning the fund to take advantage of larger trends and then, within those larger trends, picking out stocks and stock groups.

Many of the macro players started as micro investors but got too big to find investment opportunities in their traditional investment arenas, such as equities or bonds. As the funds sought ever more liquid investment opportunities, their scope of investment changed and they ended up looking for global events in which to find pricing anomalies and profit potential.

The most famous of Soros's activities – and the one that made central bankers worldwide tremble – was his investment in sterling in 1992. Recently interviewed about his activities that day, Soros described the sequence of events as knowing that he had "a kill" – not a word that would endear him to his victims of that day, but an accurate one, given the intensity of the situation.

In September 1992, Soros took on the Bank of England believing that sterling was overvalued. He shorted $10bn worth of sterling. The UK government and the Bank of England attempted to defend sterling – interest rates moved three times in one day and UK banks watched in horror as it appeared that they would be bust by the end of the day. The solution was found when the pound dropped out of the exchange rate mechanism – a step that Paul Tudor Jones II, writing in the foreword to *The Alchemy of Finance*, states "freed the English people from recession."

The Bank of England has never revealed what its losses were that day, but it is estimated that up to £15bn was spent in a futile attempt to save the pound. For his part, Soros collected $1bn and stepped into the newspapers as the man that could attempt to crash a currency.

In 1994, Soros was invited to deliver testimony to the US Congress on the stability of the financial markets, particularly with regard to hedge fund and derivative activity. Soros believed that the banking committee was right to be concerned about the stability of markets, saying: "Financial markets do have the potential to become unstable and require constant and vigilant supervision to prevent serious dislocations." However, he felt that hedge funds did not cause the instability, preferring to blame institutional investors who, he said, measured their performance relative to their peer group and not by an absolute yardstick. "This makes them trend-followers by definition," he said. Asked about the role hedge funds play in the foreign exchange markets, Soros said:

> The role of hedge funds in the foreign exchange markets is greatly exaggerated. A recent study estimates that the net turnover in the foreign exchange market (i.e., spot foreign exchange, forward contracts, futures contracts, swaps and options contracts) in the US is approximately $192bn per day. The figure for the market in the UK is approximately $300bn per day. The global net turnover of the nine largest foreign exchange markets is estimated to be approximately $946bn per day. On an average trading day in foreign exchange, our funds might engage in foreign exchange transactions having a total value of around $500m. While this number is admittedly large in absolute terms, in relative terms it is not: it would represent only about 1/1800th of the daily global trading volume. We believe that funds managed by Soros Fund Management constitute approximately 15% of the money invested in hedge funds. If this is true and if other hedge funds traded currencies to the same extent we do (which they do not), then all hedge funds in the aggregate control at most 1/180th (or 0.005) of the daily global trading volume in the foreign exchange markets.

Whatever Soros's role is in the world's markets, you can see that these macro funds are so powerful that they can be involved in the investment process way beyond the corporate level, where one might expect to find fund managers. Asked specifically if it were possible for a private investor to amass enough capital to manipulate the value of a currency, Soros replied:

> I do not believe that any market participant can, other than for a very short time, successfully influence currency markets for major currencies contrary to market fundamentals ... Hedge funds are relatively small players given the size of the global currency markets.

Soros's Quantum Fund started as a model portfolio in 1969. As he explains in *The Alchemy of Finance*:

The fund has grown from about $4m at inception to nearly $2bn and most of the growth has been internally generated. Original investors have seen the value of their shares multiply 300 fold. No investment fund has ever produced comparable results.

Writing in *Hedge Funds – An Introduction to Skill-Based Investment Strategies*, Richard Hills reports that $1000 invested at inception in the Quantum Fund, would now be worth over $2m with dividends re-invested.

Occasionally, a macro manager just calls it a day. 1995 saw one of Soros's peers, the third largest hedge fund manager in the world, Michael Steinhardt, give up trading after 28 years and returning $2.6bn to investors. He closed his four funds having achieved a compound annual rate of return of about 24% over 28 years. June 1995 saw Bruce Kovner of Caxton Corporation return some $11.6bn to investors because he felt that there was too little liquidity in the markets to trade in the way that he wanted. December 1995 found Tudor Investment Corporation returning $2bn to investors and December 1996 found Odyssey Partners closing his $1bn hedge fund.

Another macro manager whose name regularly appears in the press is Julian Robertson of Tiger Management. His funds have some $8bn under management, and like George Soros, his background lies in US equities. The Tiger Fund has achieved a return of 255.44% over the last 60 months to December 1996.

GLOBAL INTERNATIONAL HEDGE FUNDS

Established

These types of fund managers are very close to the macros. Principally, they invest in international equities in the established markets of the US, Europe and the Far East, particularly Japan. Like equity fund managers around the world, they adopt what is known as a bottom-up approach to evaluation. This means that they stock pick individual companies, looking at what they have to offer in their sector or what opportunities there are for buying or shorting. A global international hedge fund manager operating in the established markets may find a company that is not performing in line with its sector.

As an example, Julian Glatt of the Mistral European Fund, interviewed in *MAR/Hedge* March 1997, spoke of a Norwegian company, ASK, which specializes in multimedia projection equipment that links up with notebook computers for presentation purposes. At the time of the interview, Glatt reported that the company had recently demerged, and so had a very highly incentivized management team which had done relatively little outside of Norway but had great potential in the US. ASK's share price had doubled since Glatt's investment.

Emerging

Managers working in the emerging markets are not able to get such high quality research material on investment opportunities. Emerging markets are the less mature markets of the world. While they may have high growth rates, this has to be seen in the context of poor information flows, legal systems or market structures. *MAR/Hedge* lists the principal emerging market regions as:

- Asia
- Australia
- China
- Eastern Europe
- Hong Kong
- India
- Latin America
- Middle East
- Pacific Rim
- Pakistan
- former Soviet Republics
- Singapore.

A European emerging market investor, Bennett Capital Management, interviewed in *Mar/Hedge* in November 1996, reported that accounts prepared by companies headquartered in Pakistan or Egypt can look like British accounts from the 1930s. The area that this firm invests in is "roughly diamond-shaped" stretching from Poland to Pakistan to South Africa and up to Portugal. The companies are always quoted (although that may not mean the same thing in each market) and have an average capitalization of $120m. This fund manager also invests using a bottom-up approach, looking for companies that sell at a sharp discount to their cash flow. The fund manager is looking for companies that can double their cash flow in three years.

An investment that proved successful for Bennett was Egis, a Hungarian pharmaceutical company which it purchased at two and a half times earnings and saw its profitability take it up to 10 times earnings.

A prime example of how one type of hedge fund manager might invest in a wide range of investment sectors is Everest Capital which achieved significant success with holdings in emerging market debt over the first six months of October 1996. As Marko Dimitrijevic, president of Everest Capital explained in the Momentum Group's *International Hedge Fund Report III*:

The debt of the former Yugoslav republics ... was an ideal candidate for our style of investment: a misunderstood situation with low downside ... In a nutshell, as recently as March of this year, the $4.2bn in debt of what used to be Yugoslavia was available at 43 (cents on the dollar) versus a claim of principal and past due interest of 120 (cents on the dollar). We started studying the position in the Spring of 1995 and initiated positions in the Fall, after the end of the war in Bosnia, at prices in the low thirties. Because of the constant flow of television images from a very few hot spots, the perception was that the civil war in Bosnia had spread to all the territories of the former Yugoslavia. The reality is that the other four republics experienced little or no destruction and that Bosnia represented less than 10% of the GDP of the former Yugoslavia.

This was akin to the value of a holding company stock dropping by over 60% because one of its subsidiaries – contributing less than 10% of its former value – was having serious problems. In particular, we believed that the portion of the value attributable to the two northern republics, Slovenia and Croatia, was worth 48 cents on the dollar, i.e., more than we were paying for all the debt.

During the second quarter of 1996, the debt restructuring greatly accelerated and as the market realized the extent of the value and how soon it would be available, the debt moved up to over 75 cents on the dollar or a 74% appreciation in three months. By focusing on the Croatian component we actually did even better as it appreciated by over 110% during the same period. To highlight the market's misperception of this investment, Slovenia's portion received an excellent A investment grade rating from Standard & Poors. This was a very wide discrepancy between perception and reality.

Everest Capital is normally to be found in the event-driven pool of hedge fund managers, but here it made a significant return from an emerging market debt situation.

EVENT DRIVEN HEDGE FUND MANAGERS

Risk arbitrage

Event driven managers operate within the risk arbitrage sector where positions are taken to capitalize on a specific event in a company, usually connected with a restructuring or merger and acquisition activity. This is one of the few investment sectors where economic or market conditions are not a concern.

Writing in *Evaluating and Implementing Hedge Fund Strategies* (edited by Ron Lake), Richard B Nye of Baker Nye and Roy C Smith, Stern School of Business, New York University claim that risk arbitrage is about 100 years old in America. They believe that the basic principles were established in the 1890s when, during a five year depression, roughly 25% of the railroad industry went bankrupt and had to be restructured.

> Usually this involved exchanging old debt for a combination of new debt, some preferred stock and a share or two of common. These new securities often represented more value than that accorded to them by the reorganizers. As a result, arbitrageurs (then as now) could buy the old debt, and sell the new securities after a time for a respectable profit.

MAR/Hedge looks at another aspect of risk arbitrage, defining it as a manager simultaneously buying stock in a company being acquired and selling stock in its acquirers. The potential downside of this type of risk arbitrage comes if a deal fails to go through.

Distressed securities

Distressed securities, also part of the event driven sector, are companies that are in dire straits. Meaden of TASS helpfully points out: "In this context, distress means companies in need of legal action to sort them out, not companies in need of Prozac."

The hedge fund manager operating in the distressed securities arena is examining a company that is in serious re-organization or going into bankruptcy. The manager may believe that the underlying assets of the company are such that the company may emerge in better shape than the current share price would have one believe.

Distressed securities managers are often confused with short sellers. They are in fact different (distressed securities managers don't necessarily go short) but do benefit from the same market conditions – weak. As you might imagine, distressed securities managers and short sellers have had a difficult time of it during the strong equity markets of the middle to late 1990s.

The Momentum Group's *International Hedge Fund Report IV*, March 1997 carries a report on James Bennett of Bennett Offshore Investment Corporation "who explains that for a predator feeding on frail companies, the 1996 markets were unhelpful, but 1997 may prove much more toothsome:"

> The domestic (i.e., US) "Goldilocks" economy is harmful to a "Vulture's" health ... low unemployment and inflation rates have kept interest low and the stock market is on a two year roll. Since the individual cannot miss out on this investment gold rush, money is pouring into mutual funds providing tremendous liquidity to fuel stock market prices.

MARKET NEUTRAL HEDGE FUNDS

Long/short

Market neutral funds attempt to do the impossible – they try to "neutralize" market risk by simultaneously going long and short or by arbitraging. As you might imagine, they run a big risk of achieving little performance at all. Julian Glatt explains a long/short position in a *MAR/Hedge* interview in March 1997.

> In the fund, Glatt currently holds positions in 25 companies on the long side and 15 on the short. He doesn't use shorts to make money. He usually uses them to eliminate the characteristics of longs that he doesn't like. "If I liked Volvo which is being valued because it's a truck company, but I only liked the car side, I would hedge using a Swedish truck company that I don't like."

Writing in Ron Lake's *Evaluating and Implementing Hedge Fund Strategies*, Nicholas Rallis, then of IFM Asset Management, recommends that investors ask fund managers who claim that their funds are market neutral: what is the market risk to which you refer and is the claimed neutrality objective or subjective? There are many types of market risk, claims Rallis, and the investor should be clear that the one that the fund is aiming to eliminate is the one that he is most concerned about.

Bond/convertible arbitrage

Another type of fund that falls within the market neutral category is the bond fund, particularly the kind that arbitrages between convertible bonds and their underlying equities, seeking to profit from mispricing in the relationship between the two. As this sector has grown, opportunities have become more difficult to find as markets have become more efficient in their pricing. Nowadays, many of these types of funds are invested in the emerging markets. Interviewed in *Mar/Hedge* in February 1997, Gustaf Bradshaw, at the time director of research for the BAII Funds said:

The art of the convertible arbitrageur ... lies in the calculation of the amount of underlying equity that should be sold short against the local convertible position. This ratio can be adjusted depending on a manager's market view and so there is a large element of personal skill involved. "This is an area where the skill and experience of the portfolio managers are vital because the computer systems are there to be overridden by the managers," he says. Liquidity is one of the constraints in trading convertibles or warrants. "You can often see great opportunities but no exit," explains Bradshaw.

Mortgage backed securities

Another type of arbitrage fund is the mortgage backed securities fund. A specialist in this market, such as Atlantic Portfolio Analytics Management (APAM) arbitrages between the mortgage backed security market, the treasury market and the options and swaps market. Interviewed in *MAR/Hedge* September 1996, Jon Knight of APAM explained:

> "Some of the MBSs have their own derivatives, collateralized mortgage obligations or CMOs."

> We make a trade-off between uncertainty in horizon pricing versus the cheapness of the cash flows that we are buying in the mortgage market.

There is a full interview with Jon Knight of APAM in Chapter 6.

This type of trading is not common in Europe, where securitization of mortgages is not a big business. In the US and, to a much lesser extent, in the UK, government or commercial bank groups issue securities backed by pooled mortgages – hence mortgage backed securities or MBSs. Some of the MBSs are guaranteed by the issuer and they pay fixed coupons. Some of the MBSs have their own derivatives, collateralized mortgage obligations or CMOs. The MBS market is incredibly complex as new securities have arisen which allow investors to trade in interest-only strips or principal-only strips and so on. The opportunity for trade lies in the basic fact that home-owners make decisions based on all sorts of personal reasons – not necessarily market or financially driven – and so the market moves against these very complex products.

SHORT SELLERS

As mentioned in the context of distressed securities managers above, short sellers generally have a pretty rotten time of it during bull markets. The problem is partly one of their image. Gordon W Ringoen of G W Ringoen & Co writes in *Evaluating and Implementing Hedge Fund Strategies*:

> During periods of market stability short selling tends to be looked upon as representing a negative attitude and a vote against prosperity. As a market declines, a short seller is seen as a pariah who devours the wealth of the masses through predatory bear raids. During bull markets, the investment community looks on with bemusement as the short seller apparently throws away his capital while others become rich.

As explained in Chapter One, short sellers borrow stock and sell it in the expectation that the market will go down and they will be able to buy it back at a lower price. This is something of a challenge during a soaring equity market and certainly requires careful research. From 1991 to 1995 short sellers have suffered "abysmal" performance against an overall market rise of 75%. Indeed, Ringoen explains that short sellers became a target for investment decisions themselves:

> During the first half of the 1990s, publicizing the fundamental weaknesses of a hyped stock was like putting a red cape in front of the rampaging bull. A stock with a large short position which was profiled as a major position of a prominent short seller became reason enough to buy it. This was because squeezing shorts had proved to be a profitable trading tactic.

However, the bull markets of the 1980s were kinder to short sellers who thrived, largely on the back of shorting hype – expecting equities that brokers were raving about to collapse. Ringoen talks of a "legendary investor" Bob Wilson who shorted stocks hyped by brokerage firms as they rose in price. "He would then publicize the fundamental shortcomings of the stock which would contribute to the puncture of the bubble, and a rise in his fortunes."

The problems of the 1990s have diminished the sector considerably: from $3.5bn in 1990 down to "a few hundred million US dollars" according to Philipp Cottier writing in *Hedge Funds and Managed Futures*.

The real problem facing short sellers is that on a long position, potential losses are finite – a stock can only fall to be worth nothing – while on the short side, a stock's price is infinite, it has no ceiling. Careful research leading to acute stock selection is the key during bull markets. As I write this, many people predict a crash in the equity markets and if that happens, of course, the short sellers will come into their own.

PUTTING IT ALL TOGETHER

Now that we have some idea of all the different types of hedge funds available, we can look at how well they work as investment vehicles. The next chapter is dedicated specifically to the performance of hedge funds, particularly in relation to traditional investments, but here I plan to take a look at how the different investment sectors work in performance terms.

In August 1997, London-based Financial Risk Management (FRM), an independent investment advisory company specializing in absolute return investing, conducted a research study, *Hedge Fund Strategy Sector Analysis*, looking at the period June 1992 to May 1997.

FRM looked at four hedge fund sectors which they defined as tactical trading (discretionary and systematic trading), event driven, market neutral and equity and fixed-income long/short. The purpose of their analysis was to find which sectors were most suitable for investors with different risk and return investment objectives. Measurement of risk/return was achieved using the Sharpe ratio.

The Sharpe ratio

This was devised by William Sharpe, a colleague of Markowitz, and is one of the key measurement tools used in assessing the riskiness of investments. The formula for the ratio varies considerably from user to user, but *MAR/Hedge* defines it as the annualized geometric rate of return minus the rate of return on a risk-free investment divided by the annualized arithmetic standard deviation.

> The numerator shows the reward for pure risk-taking, while the denominator measures the volatility of monthly performance, an indicator of risk. The higher the Sharpe ratio, the more return per unit of risk. A Sharpe ratio of 1:1 or higher indicates that the rate of return is proportional or more than proportional to the risk run in seeking that reward.
>
> *MAR/Hedge*

The risk-free investment used by FRM is the US Treasury Bill (T-Bill). As the FRM study explains:

> US T-Bills are considered to have zero risk, and offer a consistent rate of return. To achieve higher rates of return than US T-Bills investors must accept risk. Efficient investment involves achieving the highest excess return (returns in excess of US T-Bills) for a given level of risk, or alternatively taking the least risk to achieve a certain amount of excess return. The Sharpe ratio measures how efficiently excess returns have been achieved, with higher Sharpe ratios indicating higher efficiency. A Sharpe ratio of higher than 1.0 is generally considered good. Funds with high and stable Sharpe ratios over time are most suitable because they offer investors definite advantages over less efficient investments. Improved efficiency means that a higher return can be achieved by taking the same amount of risk, or the same return can be achieved at much lower risk. This benefits investors by enabling them to select investments that best match their investment objectives and to reduce the volatility inherent in their portfolio's returns. Stable performance over time is important to ensure that efficiency is maintained and that the funds consistently meet and exceed investors' objectives.

Performance in the FRM study was charted as return versus standard deviation for the five year period June 1992 to May 1997 and for two independent 30 month time periods, June 1992 to November 1994 and December 1994 to May 1997. The same funds were used for all three periods, and the charts show the performance of indices such as the S&P 500, Lehman Aggregate, MSCI World and T-Bills for comparison purposes.

The funds analyzed by FRM were single manager funds with a five year track record which spanned June 1992 to May 1997. The funds were split into sectors based on their investment strategy, ranked by Sharpe ratio for the five year period and then the sectors divided into quartiles based on rank. Figures 3.3 to 3.16 show the results of the research.

Figures 3.3 to 3.5 show the performance of the event driven sector over three time frames. Performance is generally good and the findings show that the sector achieved the performance more efficiently than the S&P and other indices shown. FRM concludes that this sector is the more appropriate for conservative investors.

The findings for the market neutral sector, depicted in Figures 3.6 to 3.8 show that again the sector is appropriate for conservative investors, although fund selection is more important as the bottom quartile's performance is poor.

Figures 3.9 to 3.11 cover the performance of the equity and fixed-income long/short sector. Here, FRM found that the average performance of the top quartile is efficient and its performance improved when the S&P 500 performance improved. However, the bottom half of the sector did not perform well, implying that fund selection is important in this sector. FRM deems this sector as appropriate for most investors, ranging from conservative to sensibly aggressive.

Figures 3.12 to 3.14 show the performance of the tactical trading sector and here FRM found that this sector was less appropriate for many investors. 'Only the top quartile of the sector achieves acceptable performance, with funds outside this quartile performing unacceptably. Investors can achieve more efficient performance using traditional investments without the difficulty of identifying and investing in funds in the top quartile of this sector.'

Figures 3.15 to 3.16 show the comparisons between sectors.

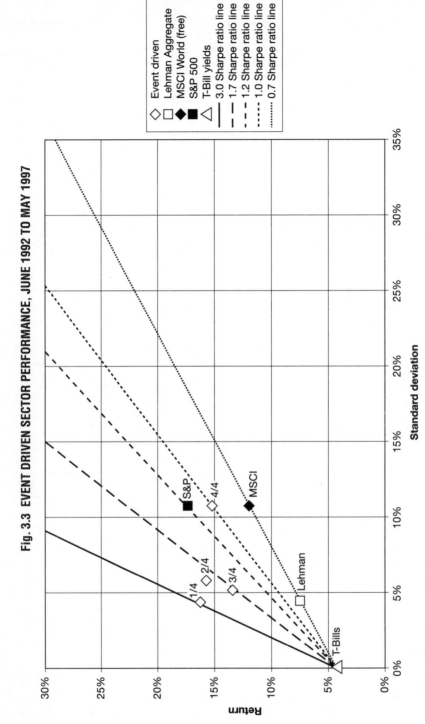

Fig. 3.3 EVENT DRIVEN SECTOR PERFORMANCE, JUNE 1992 TO MAY 1997

Source: Financial Risk Management

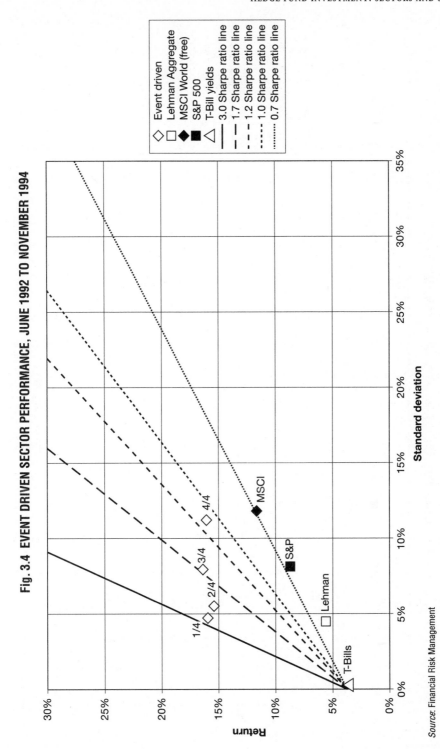

Fig. 3.4 EVENT DRIVEN SECTOR PERFORMANCE, JUNE 1992 TO NOVEMBER 1994

Source: Financial Risk Management

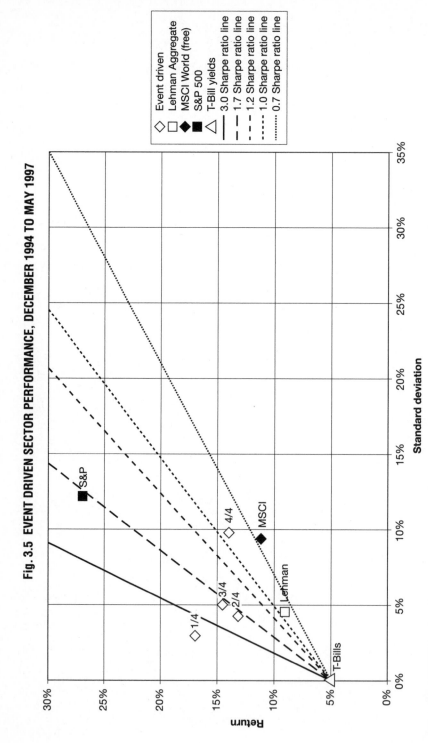

Fig. 3.5 EVENT DRIVEN SECTOR PERFORMANCE, DECEMBER 1994 TO MAY 1997

◇	Event driven
□	Lehman Aggregate
◆	MSCI World (free)
■	S&P 500
△	T-Bill yields
——	3.0 Sharpe ratio line
– –	1.7 Sharpe ratio line
- - -	1.2 Sharpe ratio line
······	1.0 Sharpe ratio line
·········	0.7 Sharpe ratio line

Source: Financial Risk Management

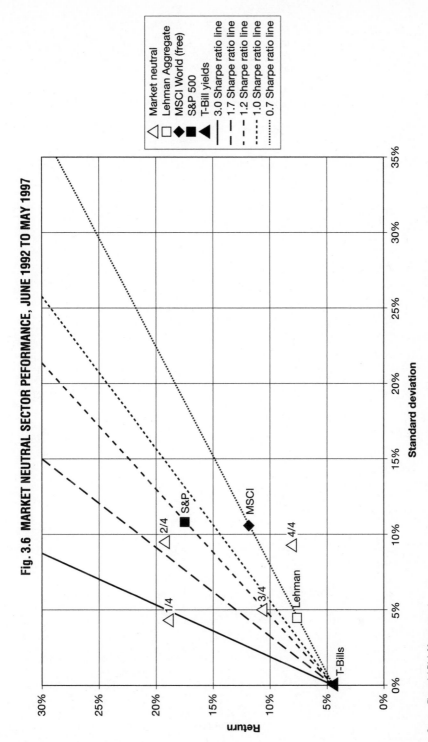

Fig. 3.6 MARKET NEUTRAL SECTOR PEFORMANCE, JUNE 1992 TO MAY 1997

Legend:
△ Market neutral
□ Lehman Aggregate
◆ MSCI World (free)
■ S&P 500
◀ T-Bill yields
— 3.0 Sharpe ratio line
– – 1.7 Sharpe ratio line
– · – 1.2 Sharpe ratio line
······ 1.0 Sharpe ratio line
·········· 0.7 Sharpe ratio line

Source: Financial Risk Management

57

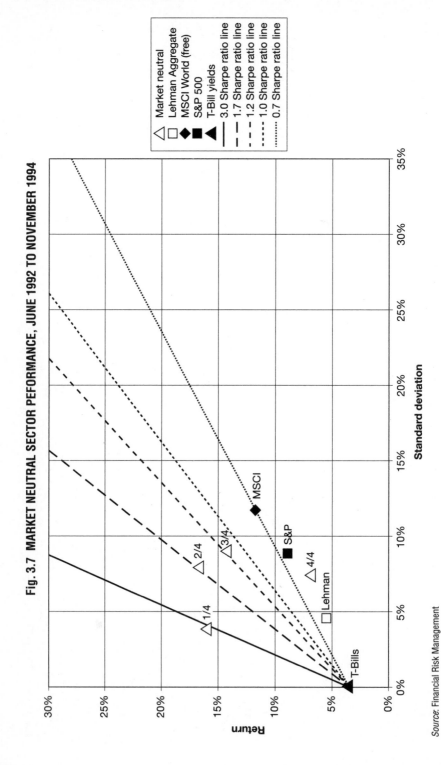

Fig. 3.7 MARKET NEUTRAL SECTOR PEFORMANCE, JUNE 1992 TO NOVEMBER 1994

Source: Financial Risk Management

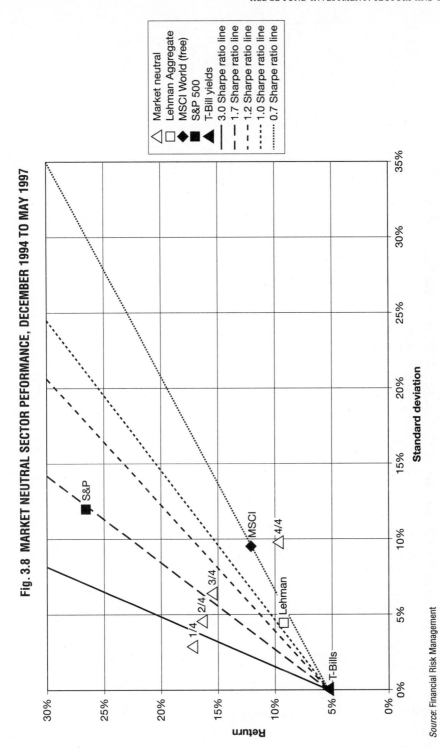

Fig. 3.8 MARKET NEUTRAL SECTOR PEFORMANCE, DECEMBER 1994 TO MAY 1997

Legend:
- △ Market neutral
- □ Lehman Aggregate
- ◆ MSCI World (free)
- ■ S&P 500
- ◀ T-Bill yields
- —— 3.0 Sharpe ratio line
- – – 1.7 Sharpe ratio line
- – – – 1.2 Sharpe ratio line
- ······ 1.0 Sharpe ratio line
- ········ 0.7 Sharpe ratio line

Return (y-axis)
Standard deviation (x-axis)

Source: Financial Risk Management

59

Fig. 3.9 EQUITY AND FIXED-INCOME LONG/SHORT SECTOR PERFORMANCE, JUNE 1992 TO MAY 1997

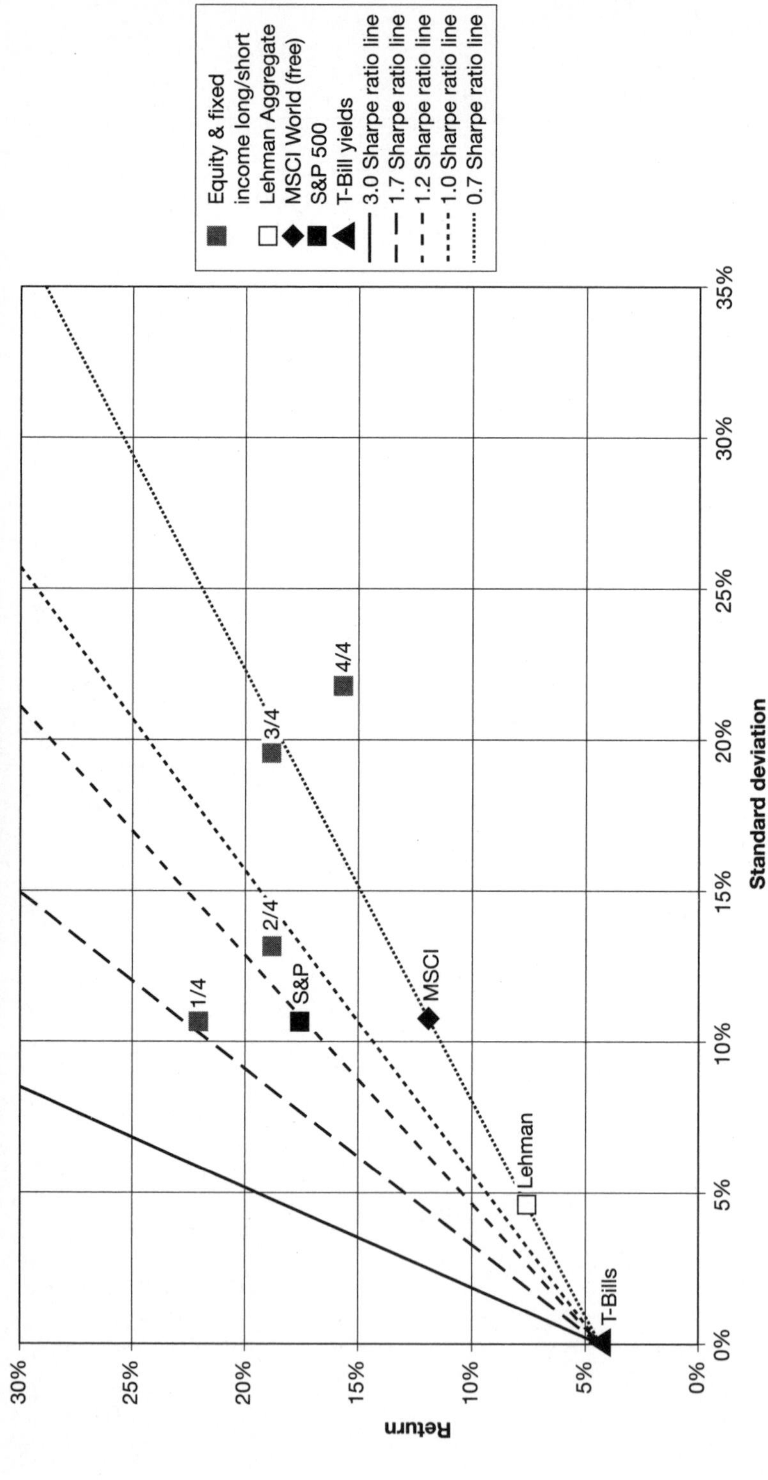
Equity & fixed income long/short
Lehman Aggregate
MSCI World (free)
S&P 500
T-Bill yields
3.0 Sharpe ratio line
1.7 Sharpe ratio line
1.2 Sharpe ratio line
1.0 Sharpe ratio line
0.7 Sharpe ratio line
Return
30%
25%
20%
15%
10%
5%
0%
Standard deviation
0%
5%
10%
15%
20%
25%
30%
35%
1/4
2/4
3/4
4/4
S&P
MSCI
Lehman
T-Bills

Source: Financial Risk Management

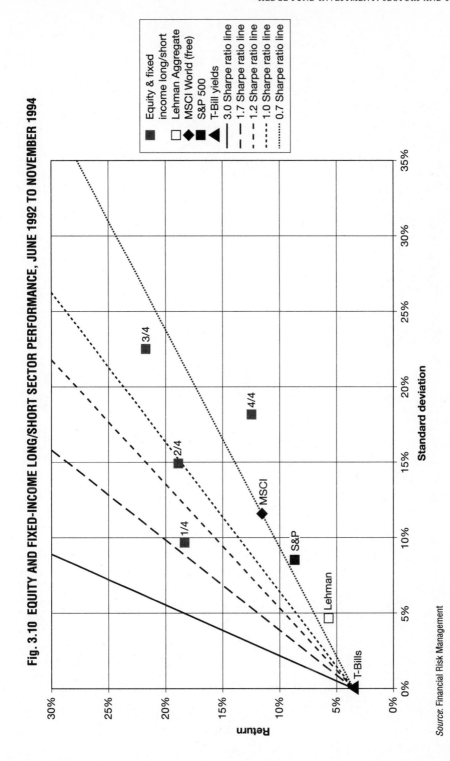

Fig. 3.10 EQUITY AND FIXED-INCOME LONG/SHORT SECTOR PERFORMANCE, JUNE 1992 TO NOVEMBER 1994

Source: Financial Risk Management

61

Fig. 3.11 EQUITY AND FIXED INCOME LONG/SHORT SECTOR PERFORMANCE, DECEMBER 1994 TO MAY 1997

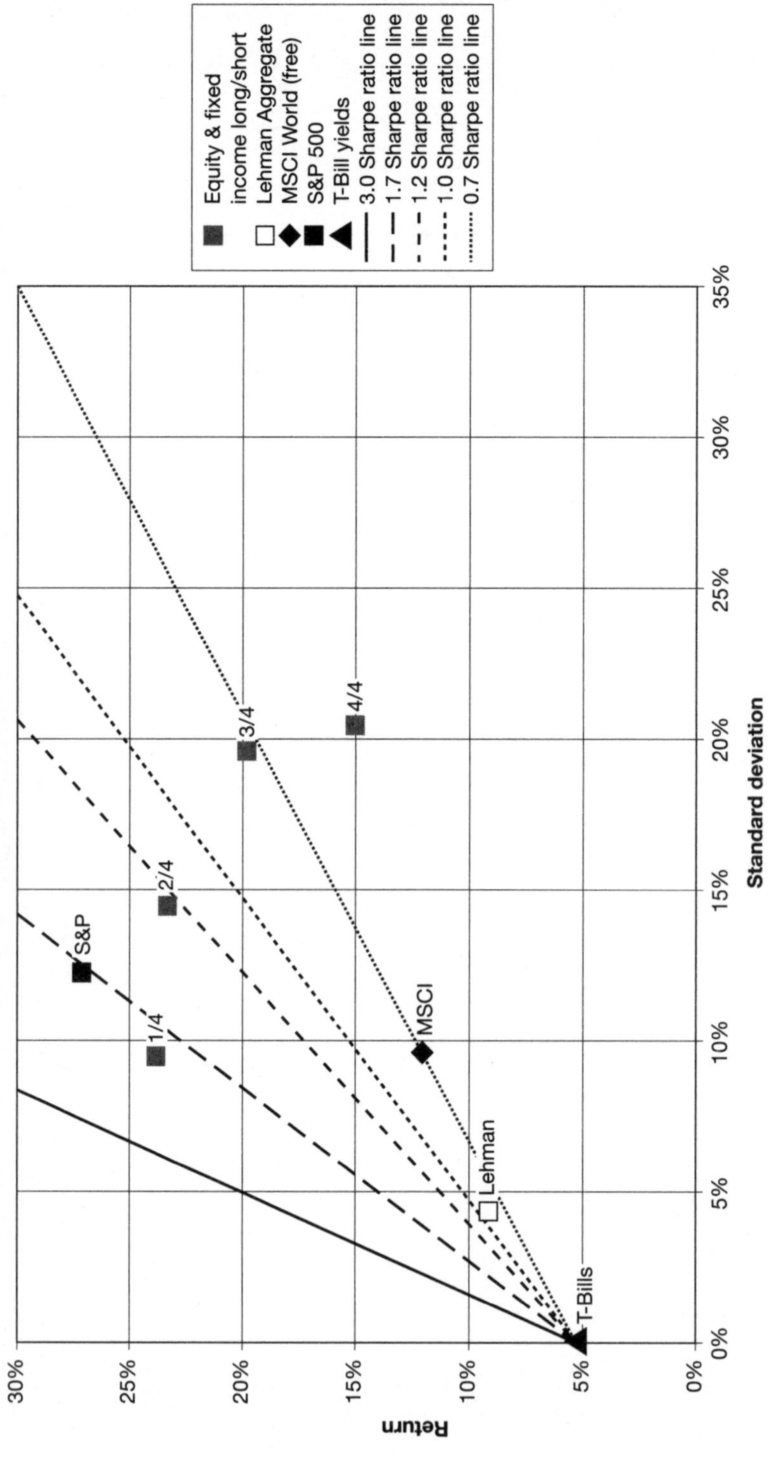
Equity & fixed income long/short
Lehman Aggregate
MSCI World (free)
S&P 500
T-Bill yields
3.0 Sharpe ratio line
1.7 Sharpe ratio line
1.2 Sharpe ratio line
1.0 Sharpe ratio line
0.7 Sharpe ratio line
Return
30%
25%
20%
15%
10%
5%
0%
Standard deviation
0%
5%
10%
15%
20%
25%
30%
35%
S&P
1/4
2/4
3/4
4/4
MSCI
Lehman
T-Bills

Source: Financial Risk Management

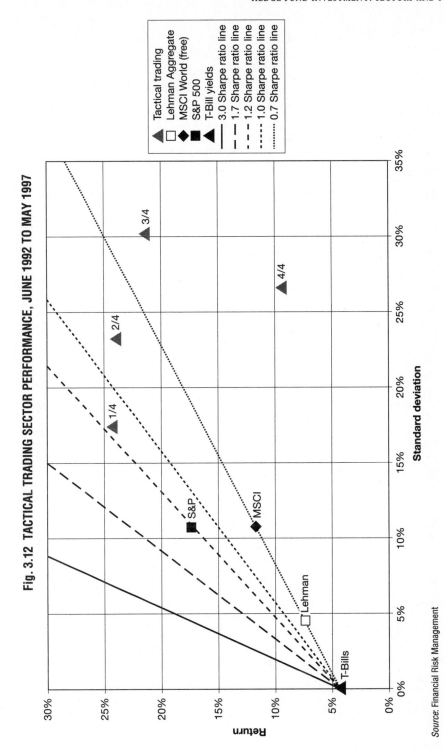

Fig. 3.12 TACTICAL TRADING SECTOR PERFORMANCE, JUNE 1992 TO MAY 1997

Source: Financial Risk Management

63

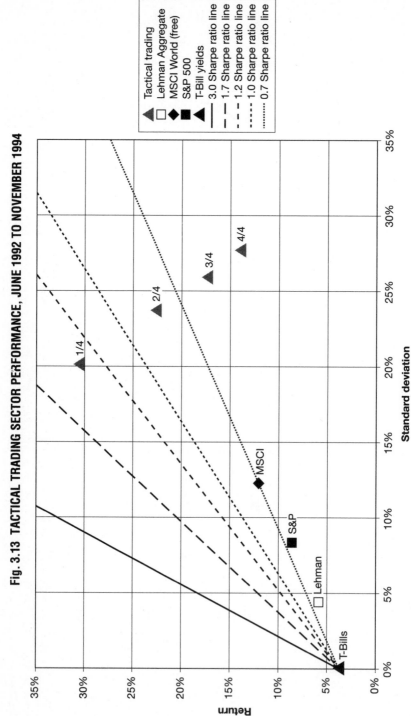

Fig. 3.13 TACTICAL TRADING SECTOR PERFORMANCE, JUNE 1992 TO NOVEMBER 1994

Source: Financial Risk Management

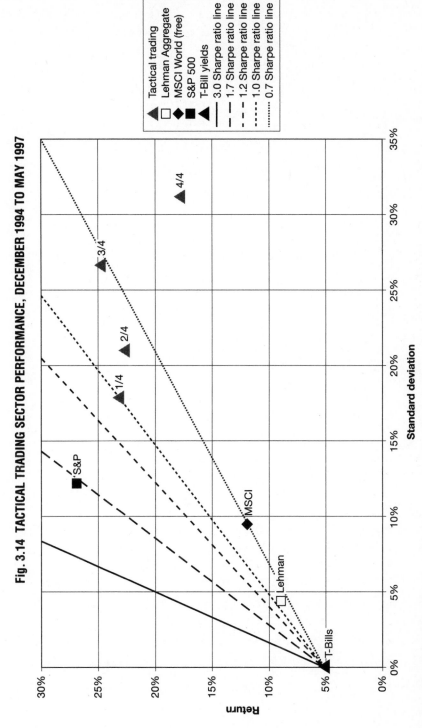

Fig. 3.14 TACTICAL TRADING SECTOR PERFORMANCE, DECEMBER 1994 TO MAY 1997

Source: Financial Risk Management

65

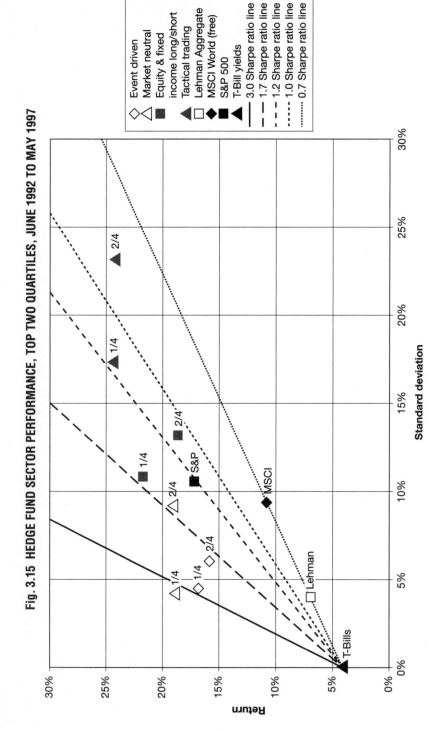

Fig. 3.15 HEDGE FUND SECTOR PERFORMANCE, TOP TWO QUARTILES, JUNE 1992 TO MAY 1997

Source: Financial Risk Management

Fig. 3.16 HEDGE FUND SECTOR PERFORMANCE, TOP QUARTILES, JUNE 1992 TO NOVEMBER 1994 AND DECEMBER 1994 TO MAY 1997

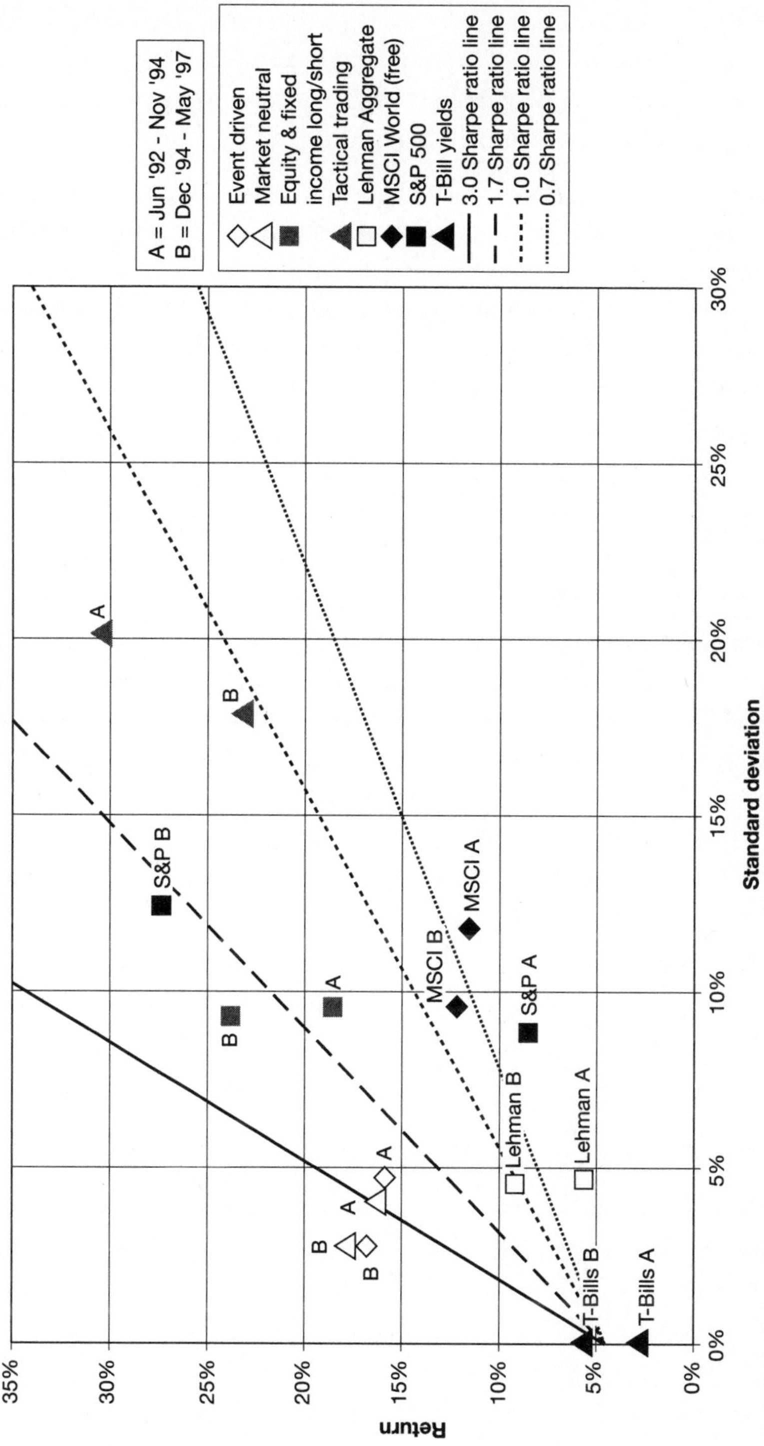

A = Jun '92 - Nov '94
B = Dec '94 - May '97

◇ Event driven
△ Market neutral
■ Equity & fixed
  income long/short
◀ Tactical trading
□ Lehman Aggregate
◆ MSCI World (free)
■ S&P 500
◀ T-Bill yields
— 3.0 Sharpe ratio line
-- 1.7 Sharpe ratio line
···· 1.0 Sharpe ratio line
···· 0.7 Sharpe ratio line

Source: Financial Risk Management

67

FRM's conclusions from the research were that the four hedge fund sectors exhibited quite different risk/return characteristics, ranging from conservative to aggressive and typically offering better returns than their indices for similar levels of risk.

Event driven and market neutral strategies offer investors the most efficient investment opportunities. The performance of the top half of the sector is significantly superior to the S&P 500 in terms of risk and return, despite the outstanding performance of the S&P 500 between December 1994 and May 1997. Equity and fixed income long/short strategies are also efficient. The performance of the event driven and market neutral strategies is stable over time, indicating that these strategies are relatively market independent. Therefore, regardless of market performance, funds in the top half of these strategies can be expected to produce efficient returns. Equity and fixed income long/short and tactical trading sectors offer opportunities for higher returns than the indices. However only the top quartile or top half of these sectors is risk/return efficient and performance stability is much lower than for event driven and market neutral sectors. To achieve the greatest benefits from investing in hedge fund strategies it is necessary to identify those fund managers who are in the top quartile or top half of their peer group. This emphasizes the importance of careful fund manager selection when making investments in hedge funds

HEDGE FUND PERFORMANCE: INVESTMENT RETURNS AND INDICES

The most exciting thing about hedge funds is their performance – when it's good, it's very good. Find out here how to identify what type of investor you are and whether hedge funds can provide the sort of returns that you seek. There are a number of sources of information on the hedge fund industry. Finally, a word on indices – they can be misleading when applied to such a diverse investment sector.

Many hedge funds achieve consistently higher performance than most traditional funds – and if you are lucky enough to spot a consistently good performer, you will receive investment returns well beyond that of equities, with little of the associated risk. Over recent years, it seems foolish to say that equities are risky but anyone who was invested through 1987 will remember how quickly a portfolio of equities can be destroyed.

According to MAR/Hedge *1997 Hedge Fund Profile*, over five years, the median returns of global macro managers have generated average returns of 19.4%, against the S&P return of 15.2% for that period, or the T-Bill rate of 4.4% for that time (see Figure 4.1). And that figure is taken during a raging bull market for equities, a market which has not shown most hedge funds in the best light. (Incidentally, Figure 4.1 shows quite clearly what happens to short sellers in raging bull markets. Not a pretty sight.)

Now we can take a look at the performance of the top performing hedge funds over 1996 (see Figure 4.2) and the least volatile funds, ranked by standard deviation (see Figure 4.3) and highest Sharpe ratio (see Figure 4.4).

Fig. 4.1 MEDIAN COMPARISONS BY STYLE

	Event driven	Global	Global macro	Market neutral	Short sellers	Fund of funds	S&P
Returns (%)							
YTD (Jan–Aug '97)	12.3	16.4	14.0	10.0	–11.3	13.2	22.9
1 year, 1996	16.9	21.2	13.4	14.6	2.8	16.7	23.0
3 year	13.4	14.4	12.8	11.7	1.5	8.7	19.7
5 year	18.3	16.1	19.4	9.1	–8.7	11.4	15.2
Standard deviation							
YTD (Jan–Aug '97)	3.5	8.1	8.1	1.0	16.2	5.5	17.8
1 year, 1996	8.1	16.8	16.2	4.8	25.1	8.8	10.9
3 year	8.6	15.8	14.0	6.0	22.2	8.8	9.7
5 year	9.1	14.3	19.4	5.8	19.4	9.1	8.7
Sharpe ratio							
YTD (Jan–Aug '97)	3.7	2.7	1.7	9.4	–1.0	2.8	1.8
1 year, 1996	1.8	1.1	0.8	2.1	–0.3	1.6	1.4
3 year	1.4	0.7	0.5	1.3	–0.2	0.5	1.3
5 year	1.7	0.8	0.9	1.1	–0.4	0.8	1.1

Source: MAR/Hedge

Note: T-Bill rates: 1 year, 1996: 5.2%; 3 years, 1994–1996: 5.1% 5 years, 1992–1996: 4.4%

Over the longer-term – five years – global macro managers have generated an annual average return of 19.4%, out-performing the S&P 500 over the same time period.

Fig. 4.2 HEDGE FUND RANKINGS, HIGHEST RETURN, 1996

Hedge fund	Return (%)	Assets Dec–96 ($M)
1. Baring Emerg. Europe (Warrant)	193.35	163.70*
2. Tradewinds Debt Strategies	145.23	43.00
3. Regent Russian Debt Fund	143.54	44.70
4. Undervalued Assets Fund (3)	142.15	44.70
5. Reindeer Capital	131.40	20.00
6. Undervalued Assets Fund (1)	127.00	44.70
7. Undervalued Assets Fund (2)	125.18	44.70
8. Blue Tiger Investment Co.	124.98	44.70
9. Firebird Fund	124.90	54.70
10. Regent Sri Lanka Fund	121.78	44.70

Source: MAR/Hedge

*Assets combine ordinary shares and warrants

Fig. 4.3 HEDGE FUND RANKINGS, LEAST VOLATILE, 1996

Hedge fund	Standard deviation (%)	Assets Dec–96 ($M)
1. Gamma	0.72	627.39
2. Coast Enhanced Income Fund II	0.77	31.10
3. Mustang Investment	1.00	45.00
4. Shetland Fund (A)	1.16	115.00
5. AIG Intl. Interest Arbitrage	1.17	48.68
6. Black Diamond Ltd	1.27	60.26
7. TQA Arbitrage Fund	1.28	63.90
8. Aetos Corp. (A)	1.35	110.70
9. Helix Convertible Opport. Fund	1.48	8.79
10. Forest Fulcrum Fund L.P.	1.50	130.10

Source: MAR/Hedge

Fig. 4.4 HEDGE FUND RANKINGS, HIGHEST SHARPE RATIO, 1996

Hedge fund	Sharpe ratio	Assets Dec–96 ($M)
1. Mustang Investment	14.65	45.00
2. Forest Fulcrum Fund L.P.	11.88	130.10
3. Forest Fulcrum Fund Ltd.	9.81	40.10
4. III L.P.	9.58	343.00
5. Shetland Fund (A)	9.46	115.00
6. JMG Capital Partners	9.34	85.00
7. The Lexington Trust	8.67	75.00
8. Shepherd Fund Ltd.	8.53	228.00
9. III Fund Ltd.	8.22	501.00
10. Stark Investments L.P.	7.92	236.00

Source: MAR/Hedge

REWARD VERSUS RISK – A DELICATE BALANCE

The fact that none of the top performing funds appears in the rankings of the other two demonstrates the world of difference between top performing and safe. As George P Van of Van Hedge Fund Advisors says:

> Investors in Soros's Quantum Fund compounded their net returns at 41% per year, over the last five years. Not bad! Investors in Askin's Granite Fund lost virtually everything when it imploded in 1994. Not good! Between these two extremes, what performance can most hedge fund investors expect? Is hedge fund "risk" as great as media reports would have us believe?

What type of investor are you?

If you are contemplating investing in hedge funds then, given their minimum investment levels, you are likely to have quite a bit of money to invest. I have heard hedge funds described as investments for people with lots of 000s. As a substantial private investor you may regard your investments in hedge funds as the froth on your portfolio, or perhaps as a small part which won't correlate with everything else.

You are quite likely to already have a sensibly constructed traditional portfolio with your assets spread among bonds, equities, cash and real estate. Perhaps your portfolio is something like the portfolios shown in the table supplied by the UK's The WM Company which shows the portfolio split of over 1500 traditionally managed UK pension funds, representing an aggregate value of £400bn (see Figure 4.5).

The tiny 0.5% next to the "Other" investment category represents the part of the pension funds' portfolios which is invested in alternative investments. (Which may explain why the alternative investment industry in Europe is not very big.)

For private investors, a recent survey conducted by the Alternative Investment Management Association (AIMA) at the 1997 Global Alternative Investment Management conference in June 1997, revealed a quite different picture. The survey found that for all types of delegates at the conference, the split is more likely to be 70% in traditional investments and 30% in alternative investments across the range of respondents, while for private investors alone, this picture reversed to 70% in alternative investments and 30% in traditional investments. But, the conference participants are not representative of the investment community in general – the fact that they were paying to attend an alternative investment management conference rather implies that they were interested in the subject. The conclusion that we can draw is that once interested in alternative investments, then investors are seriously interested.

Whatever the proportion of alternative investments in your portfolio, before you invest, you need to do some serious thinking regarding whether your alternatively invested money is money you are prepared to double or lose over the short term, or whether it is money with which you would like to achieve a slightly higher return, but not at the expense of safety.

Clearly, if you are happy to live on the edge, then the type of returns achieved by the managers in the "highest returns" table will appeal to you (see Figure 4.2 earlier).

Or maybe you are investing in hedge funds to add a different type of investment to your portfolio – something that works differently in different markets. This non-correlation argument was most effective

Fig. 4.5 WM QUARTERLY UNIVERSES: SUMMARY OF RESULTS, QUARTER 2, 1997

Investment category	Asset mix at 30/06/97			Returns – latest quarter			Returns – last 12 months		
	WM ALL Funds	WM 2000	WM 50	WM ALL Funds	WM 2000	WM 50	WM ALL Funds	WM 2000	WM 50
UK equities	52.4	54.1	51.1	4.6	4.4	4.8	20.4	19.7	21.0
Overseas equities	23.3	22.6	23.7	11.0	10.4	11.5	9.8	9.7	9.9
North America	3.7	3.1	4.2	13.9	13.8	13.9	21.6	21.6	21.6
Europe	9.3	9.9	8.8	8.4	8.2	8.6	19.7	19.3	20.0
Japan	4.4	3.8	4.8	22.5	22.6	22.5	-10.9	-9.5	-11.8
Pacific (ex Japan)	4.2	4.3	4.2	5.0	4.4	5.6	2.8	1.6	3.7
Other International	1.6	1.6	1.6	9.2	9.8	8.7	11.2	11.8	10.6
UK bonds	6.4	6.8	6.2	5.4	5.7	5.2	13.6	13.9	13.4
Overseas bonds	2.8	4.1	1.8	0.5	0.4	0.7	-2.5	-2.6	-2.3
UK index linked	4.6	3.0	5.9	1.6	1.7	1.6	9.0	9.1	9.0
Cash	5.4	6.7	4.4	0.9	1.1	0.9	4.9	4.5	5.0
Other	0.5	0.5	0.5	1.3	0.7	2.2	14.2	9.7	16.0
Total ex-property	**95.5**	**97.9**	**93.7**	**5.7**	**5.3**	**6.0**	**15.2**	**14.4**	**15.8**
UK property	4.4	2.0	6.2	3.0	2.3	3.2	11.4	9.7	11.9
Overseas property	0.1	0.0	0.2	-4.3	1.0	-5.2	-8.2	-0.1	-9.5
Total assets	**100.0**	**100.0**	**100.0**	**5.6**	**5.3**	**5.8**	**15.0**	**14.3**	**15.5**

Source: The WM Company

for the managed futures industry's search for popularity with investors. Various academic studies show that managed futures, whose underlying investments are likely to be in the commodity or financial markets, tend to work differently from equity- or bond-based investments.

This argument does not work as well for hedge funds. Partly, the diversity of their investment arenas means that they don't move together in one mass and partly because hedge funds often use a lot of equity based investments.

Most investors have some concerns about losing their money. Writing in *Evaluating and Implementing Hedge Fund Strategies*, Lloyd Hascoe and Luke Imperatore of Hascoe Associates explain their approach to investing their family's money. This is a scenario which is familiar to us all, even if we have less money to invest.

> Hascoe Associates started in the early 1980s as a result of the sale of the family's operating business. The sudden wealth created by the sale caused considerable apprehension as we were unaccustomed to managing substantial financial assets. The skills necessary to invest capital prudently are quite different than those that were required to build our operating businesses. Therefore, we were unwilling to rush into an investment programme without careful preparation. Because we knew the painstaking effort that it took for us to build wealth over many years, we decided, like many other investors of private capital, to adopt a "go slow" attitude, which resulted in us following a very methodical investment process.

GETTING INFORMATION

Information is the key to following a methodical investment process, so we can now take a brief look at performance figures and how they are arrived at and presented.

The problem with historical hedge fund data is that, as we all know, there are lies, damn lies and statistics. George P Van says:

> In predicting the future, a statistic is only as useful as:
>
> 1. The extent to which it measures that which it purports to measure
> 2. The extent to which the future replicates the past.

So while using statistics to analyze performance is not necessarily as accurate a tool as one might hope for, it's better than nothing. Van again:

> Some information, knowledgeably interpreted, is better than no information.

Historical information on hedge funds is available from a number of sources. Here is a list of the main database and research houses:

The Alternative Investment Management Association
International House
1 St Katharine's Way
London E1 9UN
Tel: 171 265 3678; Fax: 171 481 8485

Evaluation Associates Capital Markets Inc (EACM)
200 Connecticut Avenue
Suite 700
Norwalk
CT 06854
USA
Tel: 203 855 2200

Financial Risk Management
43–44 Albemarle Street
London W1X 3FE
Tel: 171 460 5250; Fax: 171 460 5251

Hedge Fund Research Inc
208 S LaSalle
Suite 774
Chicago
Il 60604
USA
Tel: 312 553 6458; Fax: 312 553 6461

MAR/Hedge

Managed Account Reports Inc
220 Fifth Avenue
19th Floor
New York
NY 1001–7781
USA
Tel: 212 213 6202; Fax: 212 213 1870
http://www.marhedge.com

MAR/Hedge is a monthly newsletter on the hedge fund industry, and the company also publishes a *Performance & Evaluation Directory* on over 1000 managers and funds of funds plus other research projects. They also organize hedge fund conferences around the world.

TASS Management Ltd

27 Palace Street
London SW1E 5HW
UK
Tel: 171 233 9797; Fax: 171 233 9159

TASS has a hedge fund database, performance analysis module and portfolio optimization program, covering the alternative investment industry. This includes hedge funds; leveraged funds; arbitrage funds; derivatives funds; managed futures funds; managed currency funds; emerging market funds and funds of funds.

Van Hedge Fund Advisors Inc

1608 Chickering Road
Nashville
TN 37215
USA
Tel: 615 377 2949; Fax: 615 373 1645

Van Hedge has a database of 2500 funds, plus information on 1500 "not yet entered" funds. They believe that they have the largest repository of hedge fund information in the world.

A WORD ON HEDGE FUND INDICES

You may think that a good indicator of the performance of hedge funds is to take a look at the indices which cover the sector and to use them as a sort of benchmark. However, the problems which face the creator of a hedge fund index are legion. Hedge funds are not static things, investing in the same portfolio year after year. While stock market indices may also be re-weighted every now and then, the difference between a hedge fund index from one month to the next could be substantial. Thomas Schneeweis, professor of finance at the University of Massachusetts' Center for International Security and Derivative Markets in the School of Management has produced a thorough guide to hedge fund indices in his paper entitled "A Comparison of Return Patterns in Traditional and Alternative Investments."

> "The problems which face the creator of a hedge fund index are legion."

Hedge fund indices differ widely in purpose, composition and weighting scheme. The major differences are in manager composition, performance determination, and style creation. Differences in composition exist because some hedge fund indices focus on a select number of hedge funds in order to better mimic a unique trading or investment style while other hedge fund providers focus on a greater sample of hedge fund managers in order to obtain a greater representative sample of the existing universe. For instance, MAR and HFR create indices from all reporting hedge fund managers as well as, in certain cases, for hedge funds whose performance is obtained from secondary sources. Sector classification is determined primarily from disclosure documents and from personal discussions with relevant hedge fund advisors. In contrast, EACM tracks the monthly performance of a smaller pre-selected set of hedge funds. MAR and HFR use the hedge fund offering memorandums and direct manager contact to determine the proper sector and subsector grouping, any may include the composite performance of several hedge funds operated by a particular manager. However, EACM reports the performance of only those funds which they are in direct contact with, and selects hedge funds for inclusion into their indices based on their knowledge of the consistency of the hedge fund's investment style with their index grouping.

MAR hedge fund indices began reporting hedge fund indices in May, 1994. While the exact composition of the MAR indices is not known, a composite of the hedge fund advisors listed in the LaPorte data system closely tracks the performance of the indices, suggesting the composition of the index is broad-based. HFR and EACM report on hedge fund index performance from 1990 to the present. However, the HFR and EACM began publishing these indices in January, 1996. As a result, the performance figures pre-1996 are subject to selection and survivor bias. Moreover, HFR will frequently revise previously reported index figures, reflecting the inclusion of new hedge funds to the index and also reflecting revised returns reported by the hedge funds themselves. EACM and MAR do not revise historical returns when altering the composition of the index.

More importantly, each hedge fund tracking firm produces indices based on different performance metrics. The MAR hedge fund indices report on the median return as well as the upper and lower quartile performance of reporting hedge fund advisors. HFR reports the mean return (unweighted) of their reporting hedge fund advisors. EACM recognizes that a lack of liquidity and fund investment rules prevent monthly rebalancing. For EACM, the initial investment is assumed to be invested with each trader for the full year. The EACM equal weighted index is rebalanced once each year. However, the EACM index is susceptible to selection bias since inclusion in the index is a subjective decision made by EACM management. Since none of the hedge funds includes the entire hedge fund universe, all have varying degrees of survivor bias, however, none of the indices recalculate historical data if a current individual hedge fund no longer reports.

In terms of portfolio construction, the decision to use a particular hedge fund index as a benchmark will probably rest on the lockup terms in the partnership documents. Since HFR and MAR indices use arithmetic averaging, which requires monthly rebalancing, to replicate, replicating this strategy requires ready access to the hedge funds, both in terms of withdrawals and new investment. Investors with long lockups would be better off tracking the EACM indices, which are based on annual lockup and which are dollar-weighted and thus require no intrayear rebalancing. In short, for any of the above indices, the MAR and HFR indices are clearly not investable, even if the composition of the index were known. The EACM index is structured to be investable, but since the index composition is not public knowledge, and no doubt many of the funds in the index are not open to new investment, there is no way for an individual to exactly replicate the index.

Towards the end of this chapter, I will take a look at other research into why hedge fund investors generally prefer to look at absolute returns rather than measure against an index.

THE JARGON

Some terms crop up regularly in assessing fund performance. The Sharpe ratio was defined in the previous chapter, but other terms that need to be explained are listed below.

Standard deviation
This is computed arithmetically and indicates to what degree each monthly return clusters about the mean. *MAR/Hedge* says that in a normal distribution, 68% of the months will be within one standard deviation of the mean and 95% will be within two standard deviations of the mean.

Alpha
This is the expected return for a hedge fund manager when the rate of return for the specified benchmark is zero. *MAR/Hedge* says this static measure reflects the value of the investment relative to the index at an instant in time.

Beta
This measures the risk or volatility of the hedge fund manager relative to the specified benchmark. Beta represents the change in return for every 1% change in the index. If the beta is more than 1, the investment typically gains or loses more than the index. In mathematical terms, beta measures the slope of the curve that portrays the investment's performance.

The Sortino ratio

Financial Risk Management, which uses the Sortino ratio in its research outlined later in this chapter, describes the Sortino ratio of an investment as constructed in an analogous way to a Sharpe ratio, but using downside deviation below a target return, instead of standard deviation as the denominator.

Drawdowns

The maximum drawdown is the greatest loss made by a fund, calculated on a peak to valley basis.

Indices versus absolute return

Hedge funds are not generally measured against an index, which makes it difficult to compare hedge funds with other types of investment. This is because hedge funds invest in such a wide variety of things in such a wide variety of styles that an index would not be comparing apples with apples. The performance of a more traditional fund, such as a global equities fund, might well be measured against a global equities index and its investment success deemed to be the degree to which it matched the index. This means, in its most extreme form, that if the index goes down 10% and the fund goes down 10% it could be considered to have achieved 100% performance.

The survey held by AIMA during the Global Alternative Investment Management Conference in Geneva in 1997 found that 64% of respondents believed that benchmarks are important, and that 40% used *MAR/Hedge* benchmarks in assessing funds. The reasons why the respondents did not use indices were also revealing as shown in Figure 4.6.

Fig. 4.6 REASONS WHY INDICES WERE NOT USED

Managers target absolute returns	36%
Not relevant	26%
Not suitable	19%
Not true measure of potential performance	15%
Understate volatility, risk and correlations	4%

Source: AIMA Survey

Downside deviation

A risk measure similar to standard deviation, says Financial Risk Management. This is based on the premise that only volatility below the investor's minimum acceptable return counts as a risk. It measures the dispersion of monthly returns below this minimum acceptable return. For FRM's research, which follows later in this chapter, zero return is used as the minimum acceptable return.

The search for low volatility

To go back to Markowitz again: he believed that portfolios that combined the best holdings with the least variance were efficient. So, least variance, lower volatility in other words, is usually considered something to be desired in building a portfolio.

Peter L Bernstein in *Against the Gods* says:

> ... volatility, or variance, has an intuitive appeal as a proxy for risk. Statistical analysis confirms what intuition suggests: most of the time, an increase in volatility is associated with a decline in the price of the asset. Moreover, our gut tells us that uncertainty should be associated with something whose value jumps around a lot over a wide range Most assets whose value is given to springing up violently tend to collapse with equal violence.

Risk-averse investors tend to look for least volatile investments.

THE RESEARCH

Financial Risk Management carried out a study into the performance characteristics of absolute return strategies as demonstrated by actively managed hedge funds.

FRM looked at funds drawn from the following sectors:

- equity long/short
- long bias equity
- event driven
- market neutral
- tactical trading.

These sectors were looked at over three, four and five year time periods and ranked by a multi-statistic ranking process. The funds ranked in the top 50% of each sector were then selected for further analysis. The selected funds were then analyzed in terms of the following measures: return, using arithmetic return; consistency, using standard deviation; risk, using downside deviation; efficiency, using both the Sharpe and the Sortino ratios and correlations, using appropriate benchmarks.

Table 1 in Figure 4.7 shows the achieved performance characteristics of each strategy group and Table 2 shows the correlation of each group to an appropriate index averaged over all time periods. In Table 2, the equity long/short and long bias equity groups were compared with the S&P 500 while the event driven and market neutral groups were compared with the JP Morgan Global Bond Index. The tactical trading group was compared with a general benchmark, the MSCI World Index.

For the sake of comparison, the performance of six benchmark indices over the same date ranges are presented in Table 3. See Figures 4.8 to 4.13.

The study found that absolute return funds outperformed standard benchmark indices in terms of risk, consistency and efficiency.

Fig. 4.7 THE PERFORMANCE CHARACTERISTICS OF ABSOLUTE RETURN FUNDS

Table 1

Parameter	Equity long/short	Long bias equity	Event driven	Market neutral	Tactical trading
Arithmetic return					
Mean	21.38%	23.47%	17.30%	13.83%	22.80%
Median	20.68%	20.94%	16.38%	12.91%	22.32%
Maximum	60.48%	48.50%	29.69%	33.56%	42.11%
Minimum	6.63%	12.93%	10.12%	5 65%	11.06%
Standard deviation					
Mean	12.71%	16.46%	5.52%	4.76%	18.87%
Median	11.37%	15.18%	5.48%	3 .95%	18.40%
Maximum	35.47%	31.78%	10.28%	14.63%	35.89%
Minimum	3.02%	10.20%	1.62%	0.94%	9.04%
Downside deviation					
Mean	5.00%	7.09%	1.49%	1.89%	7.66%
Median	4.58%	6.88%	1.58%	1.59%	7.50%
Maximum	12.33%	13.94%	3.62%	5.94%	14.36%
Minimum	0.59%	4.00%	0.21%	0.00%	4.62%

Table 1 (continued)

Sharpe ratio					
Mean	1.43	1.22	2.47	2.12	0.99
Median	1.29	0.93	2.34	1.89	0.88
Maximum	3.74	2.32	4.78	6.50	2.02
Minimum	0.58	0.76	1.54	0.65	0.56
Sortino ratio					
Mean	4.35	2.95	11.70	27.36	2.45
Median	3.16	1.78	8.84	4.21	2.06
Maximum	36.68	6.69	59.47	1000.00	5.62
Minimum	1.04	1.34	3.92	1.50	0.98
Best 12 month return					
Mean	45.34%	50.63%	29.92%	23.51%	62.49%
Median	40.44%	48.71%	29.20%	17.77%	63.77%
Worst 12 month return					
Mean	-0.52%	-1.72%	6.83%	5.00%	-6.41%
Median	-0.47%	-1.30%	6.64%	4.55%	-6.11%

Table 2

Parameter	Equity long/short	Long bias equity	Event driven	Market neutral	Tactical trading
	S&P 500	S&P 500	JPM Global Bench.	JPM Global Bench.	MSCI World
Correlation coefficient					
Average	0.35	0.43	0.11	0.16	0.09
Median	0.36	0.44	0.12	0.17	0.01
Maximum	0.80	0.73	0.37	0.45	0.61
Minimum	-0.30	0.04	-0.09	-0.10	-0.26

Table 3

Fig. 4.7 THE PERFORMANCE CHARACTERISTICS OF ABSOLUTE RETURN FUNDS (continued)

	Time period	S&P 500	MSCI World Grs	MSCI EAFE	MSCI EMF	JP Morgan Global	JP Morgan US Bench
Arithmetic return	Mar 91 – Feb 96	15.50%	10.74%	6.09%	17.85%	9.69%	8.33%
	Mar 92 – Feb 96	15.10%	12.99%	9.89%	11.19%	9.45%	7.52%
	Mar 93 – Feb 96	16.53%	16.91%	15.33%	16.52%	10.48%	5.70%
Standard deviation	Mar 91 – Feb 96	11.07%	11.92%	15.74%	21.41%	7.82%	5.20%
	Mar 92 – Feb 96	9.14%	11.42%	16.07%	20.20%	6.88%	5.35%
	Mar 93 – Feb 96	9.70%	12.11%	16.66%	22.46%	6.19%	5.33%
Downside deviation	Mar 91 – Feb 96	5.59%	7.38%	10.65%	11.36%	4.71%	3.17%
	Mar 92 – Feb 96	4.91%	6.64%	9.80%	12.26%	4.14%	3.41%
	Mar 93 – Feb 96	5.24%	6.44%	9.08%	12.22%	3.28%	3.72%
Sharpe ratio	Mar 91 – Feb 96	1.00	0.53	0.10	0.63	0.67	0.75
	Mar 92 – Feb 96	1.19	0.76	0.35	0.34	0.75	0.61
	Mar 93 – Feb 96	1.24	1.02	0.65	0.53	0.96	0.22
Sortino ratio	Mar 91 – Feb 96	1.98	0.85	0.15	1.18	1.12	1.23
	Mar 92 – Feb 96	2.21	1.32	0.57	0.57	1.25	0.95
	Mar 93 – Feb 96	2.29	1.92	1.19	0.98	1.81	0.31

Source: Financial Risk Management

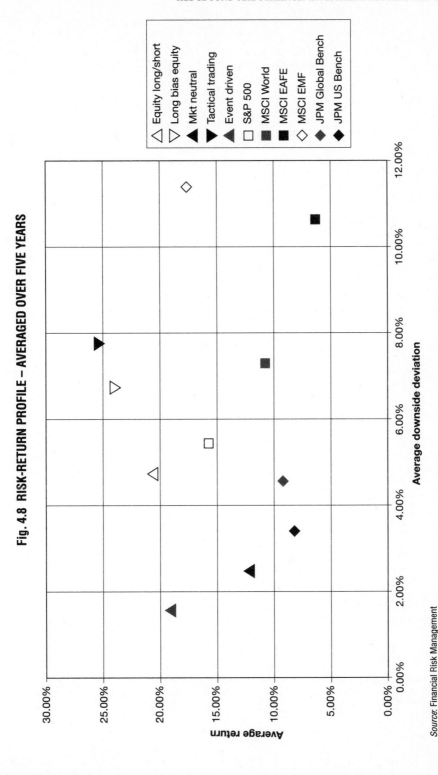

Fig. 4.8 RISK-RETURN PROFILE – AVERAGED OVER FIVE YEARS

Source: Financial Risk Management

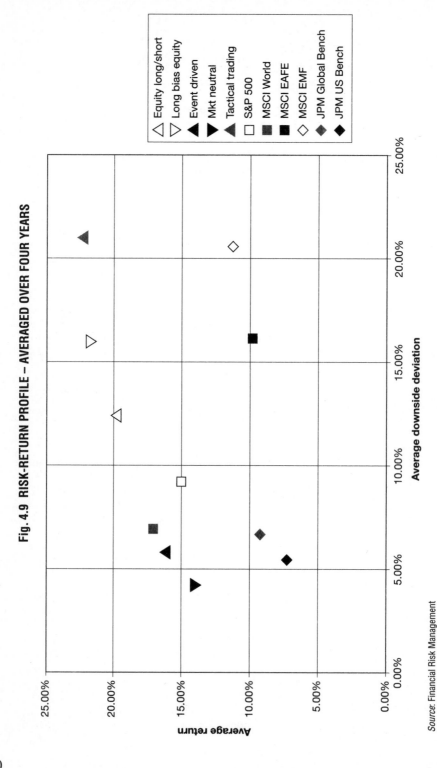

Fig. 4.9 RISK-RETURN PROFILE – AVERAGED OVER FOUR YEARS

Source: Financial Risk Management

90

Fig. 4.10 RISK-RETURN PROFILE – AVERAGED OVER THREE YEARS

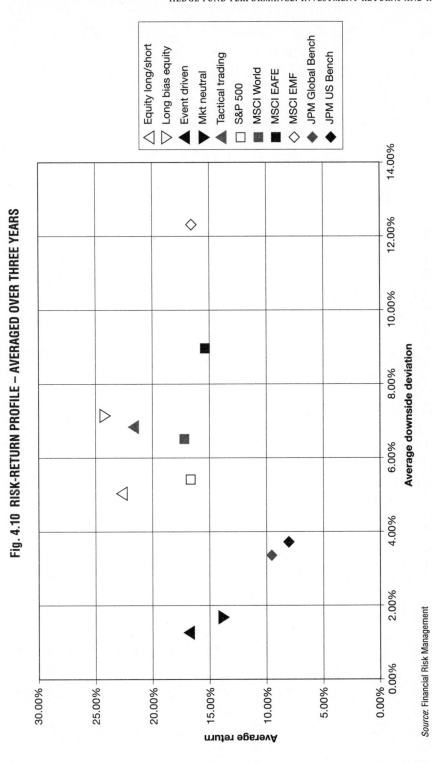

Source: Financial Risk Management

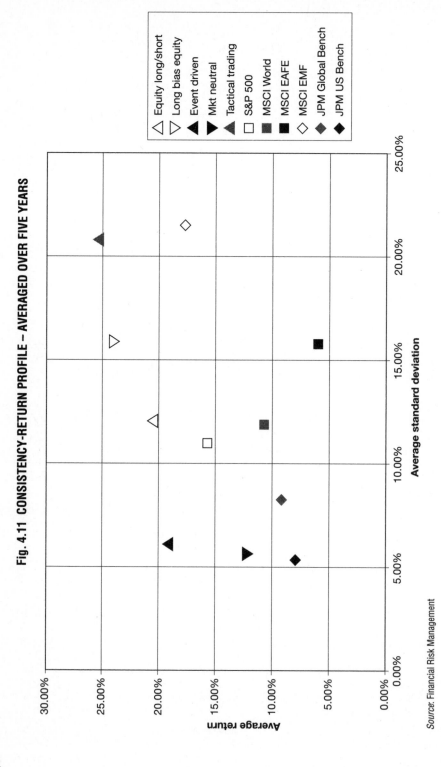

Fig. 4.11 CONSISTENCY-RETURN PROFILE – AVERAGED OVER FIVE YEARS

Average standard deviation

Average return

◁ Equity long/short
▽ Long bias equity
◀ Event driven
▶ Mkt neutral
◀ Tactical trading
☐ S&P 500
■ MSCI World
■ MSCI EAFE
◇ MSCI EMF
◆ JPM Global Bench
◆ JPM US Bench

Source: Financial Risk Management

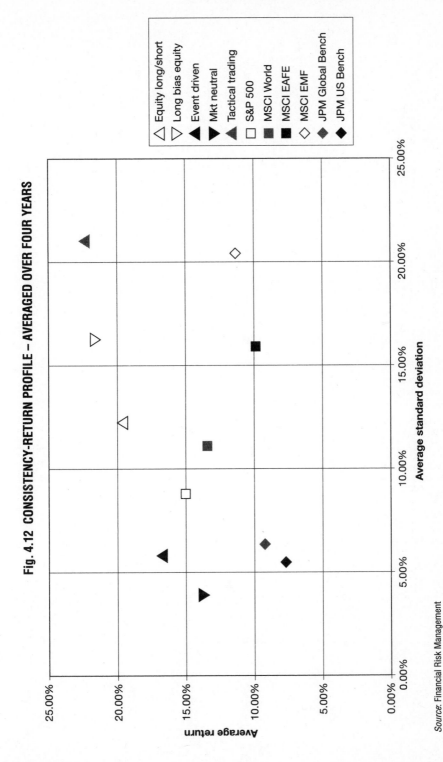

Fig. 4.12 CONSISTENCY-RETURN PROFILE – AVERAGED OVER FOUR YEARS

Source: Financial Risk Management

Fig. 4.13 CONSISTENCY-RETURN PROFILE – AVERAGED OVER THREE YEARS

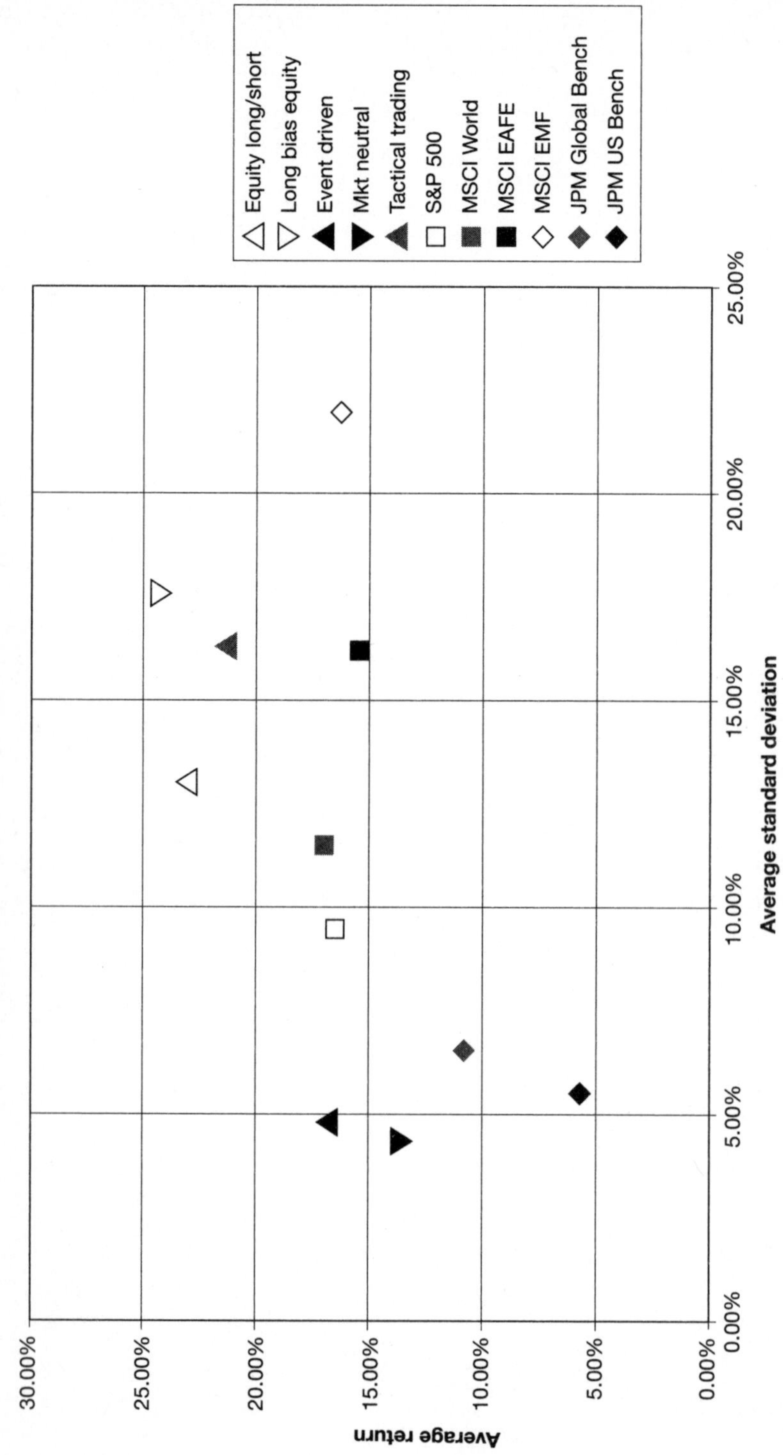

Legend:
△ Equity long/short
▽ Long bias equity
◀ Event driven
▶ Mkt neutral
◀ Tactical trading
□ S&P 500
■ MSCI World
■ MSCI EAFE
◇ MSCI EMF
◆ JPM Global Bench
◆ JPM US Bench

Source: Financial Risk Management

94

Research undertaken by Financial Risk Management comparing traditional investments and hedge funds from June 1992 to May 1997 also demonstrated the superior returns of hedge funds.

For this study, Financial Risk Management constructed two hedge fund portfolios from funds identified, outside the study period, between June 1990 and May 1992. HF Portfolio One was constructed with funds from all sectors. HF Portfolio Two was constructed with funds from only the two most efficient risk/return sectors, i.e. market neutral and event driven. See Figure 4.14.

> "Research undertaken by Financial Risk Management also demonstrated the superior returns of hedge funds."

Fig. 4.14 COMPOSITION OF HEDGE FUND PORTFOLIOS

HF portfolio	Market neutral	Event driven	Equity and fixed income long/short	Tactical trading
HF Portfolio One	25%	25%	25%	25%
HF Portfolio Two	50%	50%	–	–

Source: Financial Risk Management

These portfolios were then evaluated against a portfolio of traditional investments for the period June 1992 to May 1997. The traditional investments were represented by a customized index made up of 40% of the S&P 500, 40% of the Lehman Aggregate, 10% of the FT World and 10% of the Russell 2000, re-balanced annually. The effect of incorporating hedge funds into traditional investment portfolios was investigated by reallocating 10%, 25% and 50% of traditional index assets to the hedge fund portfolios to form six composite portfolios.

The first part of the study showed that both of the hedge fund portfolios outperformed the index, particularly in terms of lower downside deviation and fared better than the index in its losing periods. They also exhibited low and stable correlation to the index. Furthermore, for HF Portfolio One, the reduction in its downside deviation was not even at the expense of reduced annualized returns. See Figures 4.15 to 4.17.

95

Fig. 4.15 PART ONE: INDEX VS HF PORTFOLIOS – PERFORMANCE RESULTS

June 92 – May 97	Annualised return		Standard deviation		Downside deviation		Sharpe ratio	Correlation to index
	Result	Improvement	Result	Improvement	Result	Improvement		
Index	13.46%	–	7.26%	–	3.24%	–	1.24	–
HF Portfolio One	16.95%	349 bp	5.05%	221 bp	1.27%	193 bp	2.48	0.38
HF Portfolio Two	13.04%	–42 bp	2.88%	438 bp	0.42%	278 bp	2.98	0.39

Source: Financial Risk Management

Fig. 4.16 PART ONE: INDEX VS HF PORTFOLIOS – INDEX DRAWDOWNS

Index losses	Loss incurred	Index drawdown period	Recovery period	Total period of capital depreciation	HF Portfolio One		HF Portfolio Two	
					Equivalent return	Improvement	Equivalent return	Improvement
Largest	5.78%	Jan 94 – Jun 94	8 months	13 months	2.35%	813 bp	–0.35%	543 bp
2nd Largest	3.03%	Jun 96 – Jul 96	2 months	3 months	–2.33%	70 bp	0.62%	365 bp
3rd Largest	2.80%	Feb 97 – Mar 97	1 month	2 months	–0.83%	197 bp	0.32%	212 bp

Source: Financial Risk Management

Fig. 4.17 PART ONE: INDEX VS HF PORTFOLIOS – HEDGE FUND PORTFOLIO DRAWDOWNS

HF portfolio	Largest loss incurred	HF portfolio drawdown period	Recovery period	Total period of capital depreciation	Equivalent index return
HF Portfolio One	2.33%	Jun 96 – Jul 96	2 months	3 months	–3.03%
HF Portfolio Two	1.12%	Feb 94 – May 94	4 months	7 months	–2.56%

Source: Financial Risk Management

Fig. 4.18 PART TWO: COMPOSITES OF INDEX AND HF PORTFOLIOS – PERFORMANCE RESULTS

June 92 – May 97	Annualised return		Standard deviation		Downside deviation		Sharpe ratio
	Result	Improvement	Result	Improvement	Result	Improvement	
Index	13.46%	–	7.26%	–	3.24%	–	1.24
Composite One	14.39%	93 bp	7.12%	14 bp	3.06%	18 bp	1.40
Composite Two	14.00%	54 bp	7.01%	25 bp	3.02%	22 bp	1.36
Composite Three	14.46%	100 bp	5.77%	149 bp	2.31%	93 bp	1.73
Composite Four	13.30%	–16 bp	5.40%	186 bp	2.12%	112 bp	1.64
Composite Five	15.17%	171 bp	5.11%	215 bp	1.87%	137 bp	2.10
Composite Six	13.23%	–23 bp	4.34%	292 bp	1.45%	179 bp	2.02

Source: Financial Risk Management

Fig. 4.19 PART TWO: COMPOSITES OF INDEX AND HF PORTFOLIOS – INDEX DRAWDOWNS

Index losses	Index loss	Total period of capital depreciation	Composite One		Composite Two		Composite Three	
			Equivalent return	Improvement	Equivalent return	Improvement	Equivalent return	Improvement
Largest	5.78%	**13 months**	–5.05%	73 bp	–5.31%	47 bp	–3.38%	240 bp
2nd largest	3.03%	3 months	–3.16%	–13 bp	–2.86%	17 bp	–2.73%	30 bp
3rd largest	2.80%	2 months	–2.75%	5 bp	–2.63%	17 bp	–2.19%	61 bp

Fig. 4.19 PART TWO: COMPOSITES OF INDEX AND HF PORTFOLIOS – INDEX DRAWDOWNS (continued)

Index losses	Index loss	Total period of capital depreciation	Composite Four		Composite Five		Composite Six	
			Equivalent return	Improvement	Equivalent return	Improvement	Equivalent return	Improvement
Largest	5.78%	**13 months**	-4.16%	162 bp	-1.78%	400 bp	-3.07%	271 bp
2nd largest	3.03%	3 months	-1.84%	119 bp	-2.61%	42 bp	-1.14%	189 bp
3rd largest	2.80%	2 months	-1.85%	95 bp	-1.80%	100 bp	-1.23%	157 bp

Source: Financial Risk Management

Fig. 4.20 PART TWO: COMPOSITES OF INDEX AND HF PORTFOLIOS – COMPOSITE DRAWDOWNS

Composites	Composite largest loss	Drawdown period	Recovery period	Total period of capital depreciation	Equivalent index return
Composite One	5.17%	Jan 94 – Mar 94	11 months	**13 months**	-5.52%
Composite Two	5.31%	Jan 94 – Jun 94	8 months	**13 months**	-5.78%
Composite Three	4.08%	Jan 94 – Mar 94	5 months	**7 months**	-5.52%
Composite Four	4.16%	Jan 94 – Jun 94	8 months	**13 months**	-5.78%
Composite Five	3.13%	Jan 94 – Mar 94	5 months	**7 months**	-5.52%
Composite Six	3.07%	Jan 94 – Jun 94	2 months	**7 months**	-5.78%

Source: Financial Risk Management

FRM reports:

Secondly, the analysis of the composite portfolios showed that combining the index with the hedge fund portfolios resulted in improved risk-adjusted performance. The largest improvements were achieved with the largest allocations of assets to the hedge fund portfolios. The most notable performance improvements were in terms of annualized returns and downside deviation, which implies that both return and risk characteristics were improved by allocating assets to hedge funds. Losses incurred during losing periods were significantly reduced for the composites. For three of the six composites the period from the start of the largest losing period until all losses had been recouped was reduced by six months compared to the index. (See Figures 4.18 to 4.20.)

A further study conducted by Financial Risk Management examined the performance characteristics of traditional equity and absolute return funds investing in North America. This study used funds investing in the US drawn from the Micropal database as its traditional funds and hedge funds from the FRM database. All funds were ranked by Sortino ratio over the 70 month time period 1 January 1990 to 31 October 1995. The 20 funds with the highest Sortino ratios in each of the groups were selected and further analyzed in terms of return, consistency, risk, efficiency and correlations. The analysis revealed that in terms of returns, the hedge funds outperformed the long-only funds with an arithmetic mean return of 22.89% for US hedge funds, compared with 19.82% for North American Equity Funds. When each of the fund groups were ranked by return and then compared, hedge funds out-performed long-only funds 15 times out of 20 (see Figure 4.21).

In terms of consistency, the hedge funds showed far more consistency in their returns, reports FRM, as they tend to have lower standard deviations and higher proportions of gaining months and quarters than long-only funds (see Figures 4.22 to 4.24).

Furthermore, the study found that hedge funds had lower downside deviations (see Figure 4.25) and smaller drawdowns (see Figure 4.26) demonstrating their greater ability to manage risk.

US hedge funds also enjoyed the highest Sharpe and Sortino ratios (see Figures 4.27 and 4.28).

Hedge funds tended to have a lower degree of correlation with the S&P 500 than the long-only funds (see Figure 4.29).

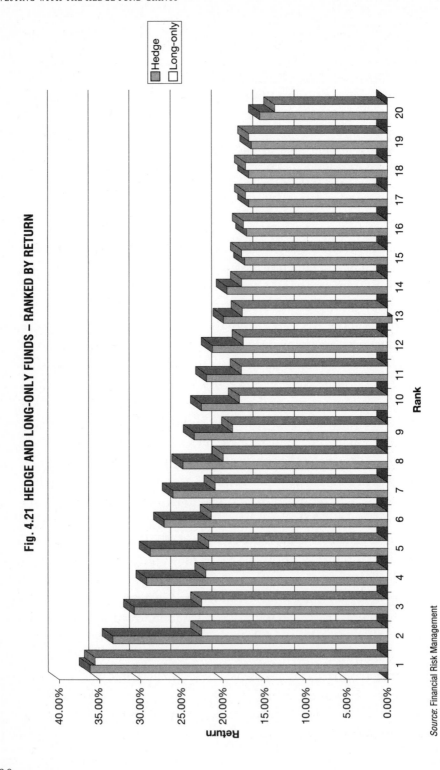

Fig. 4.21 HEDGE AND LONG-ONLY FUNDS – RANKED BY RETURN

Source: Financial Risk Management

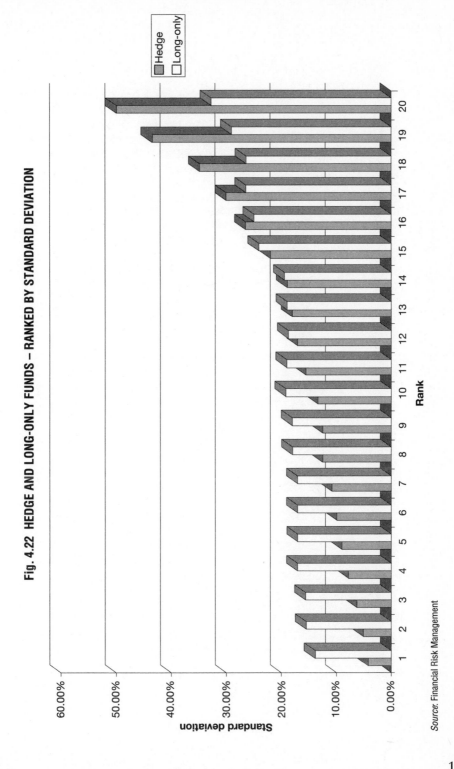

Fig. 4.22 HEDGE AND LONG-ONLY FUNDS – RANKED BY STANDARD DEVIATION

Source: Financial Risk Management

Fig. 4.23 HEDGE AND LONG-ONLY FUNDS – RANKED BY % UP MONTHS

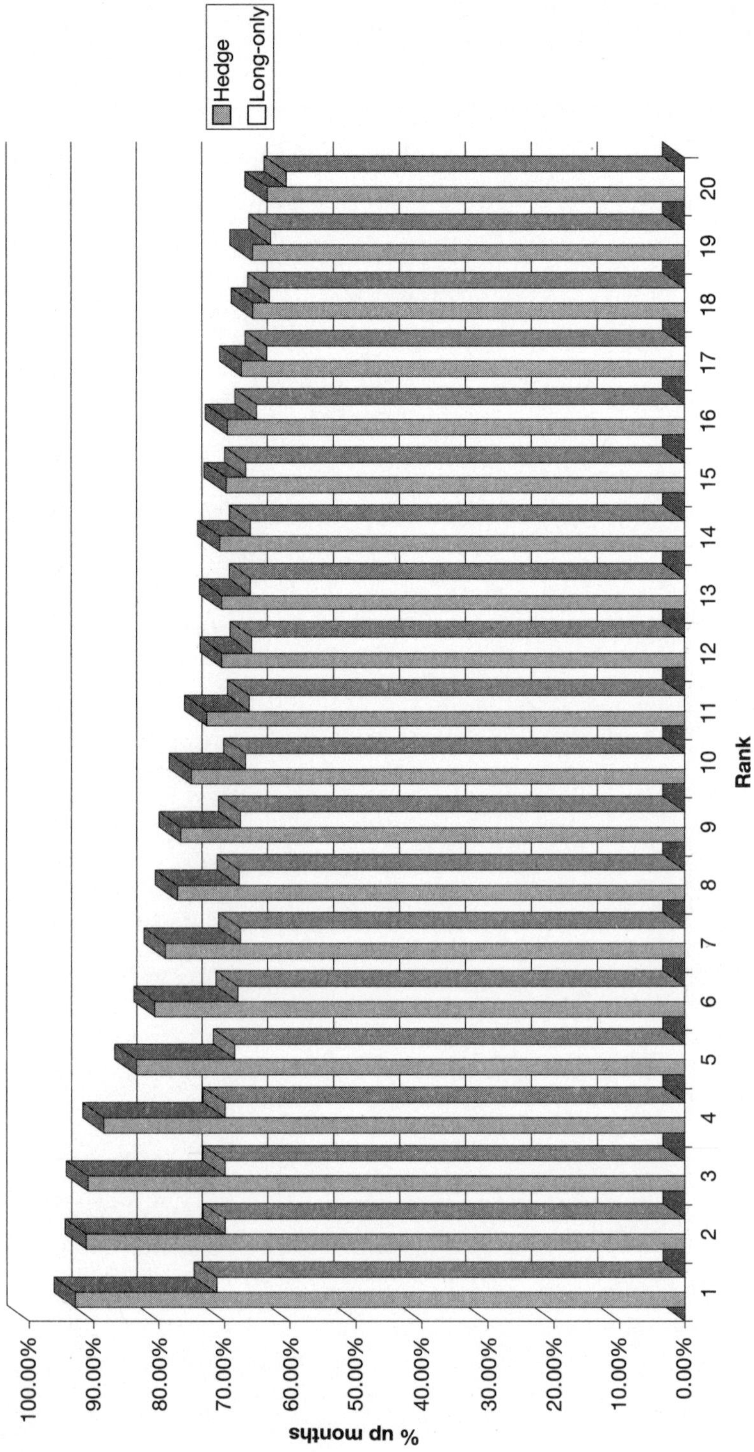

Source: Financial Risk Management

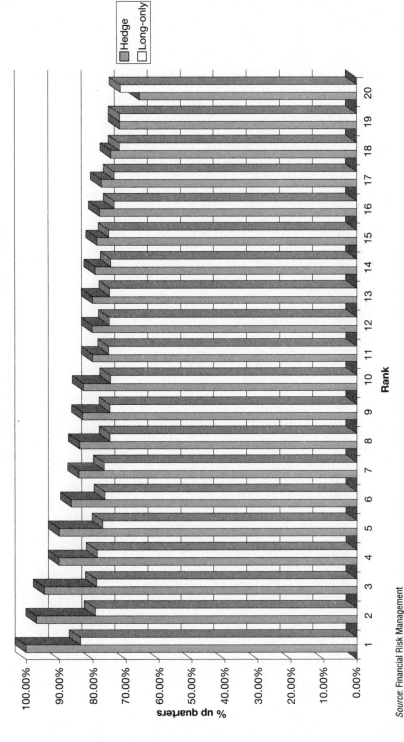

Fig. 4.24 HEDGE AND LONG-ONLY FUNDS – RANKED BY % UP QUARTERS

Source: Financial Risk Management

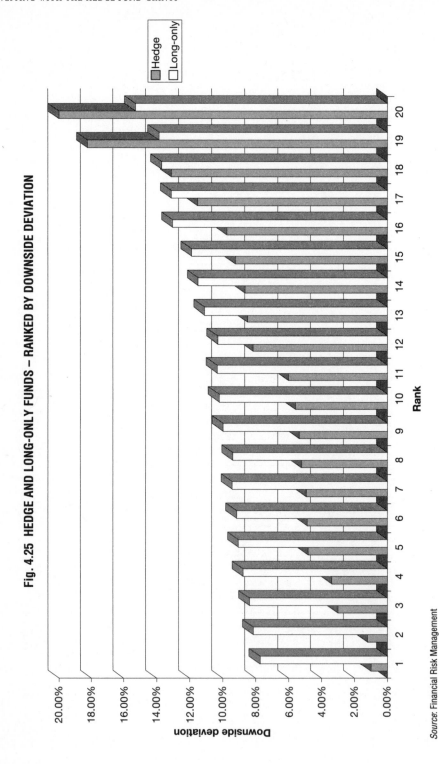

Fig. 4.25 HEDGE AND LONG-ONLY FUNDS – RANKED BY DOWNSIDE DEVIATION

Source: Financial Risk Management

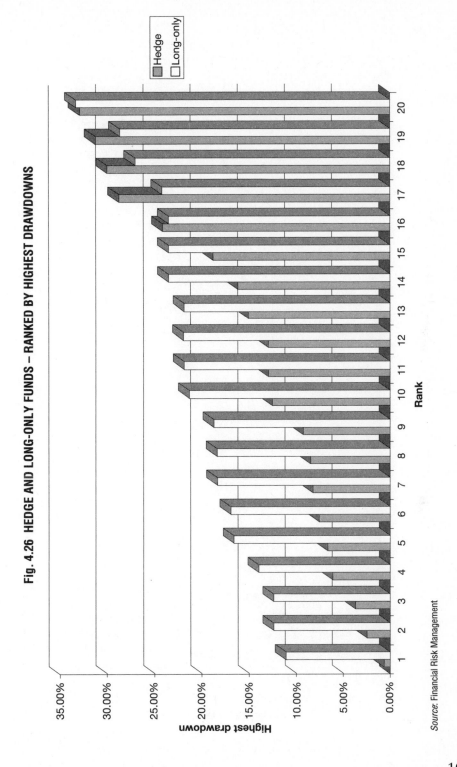

Fig. 4.26 HEDGE AND LONG-ONLY FUNDS – RANKED BY HIGHEST DRAWDOWNS

Source: Financial Risk Management

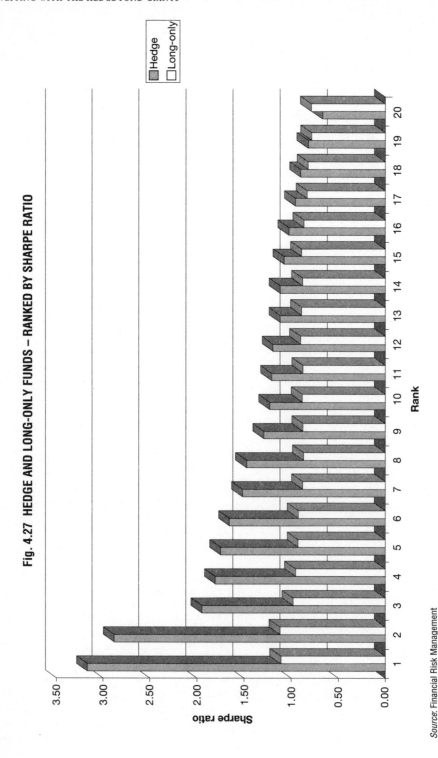

Fig. 4.27 HEDGE AND LONG-ONLY FUNDS – RANKED BY SHARPE RATIO

Source: Financial Risk Management

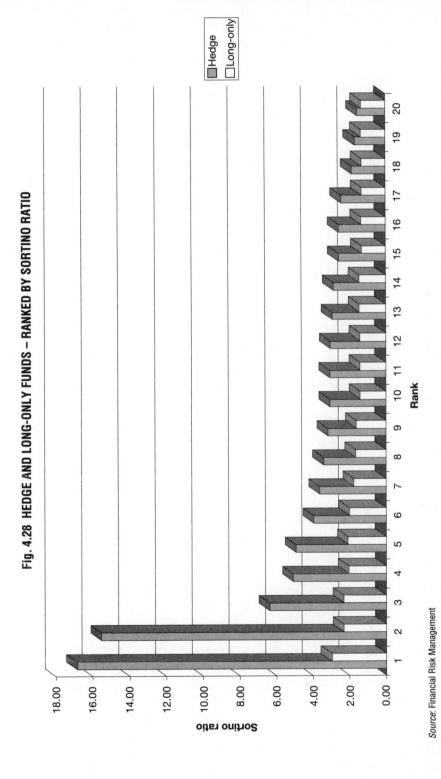

Fig. 4.28 HEDGE AND LONG-ONLY FUNDS – RANKED BY SORTINO RATIO

Source: Financial Risk Management

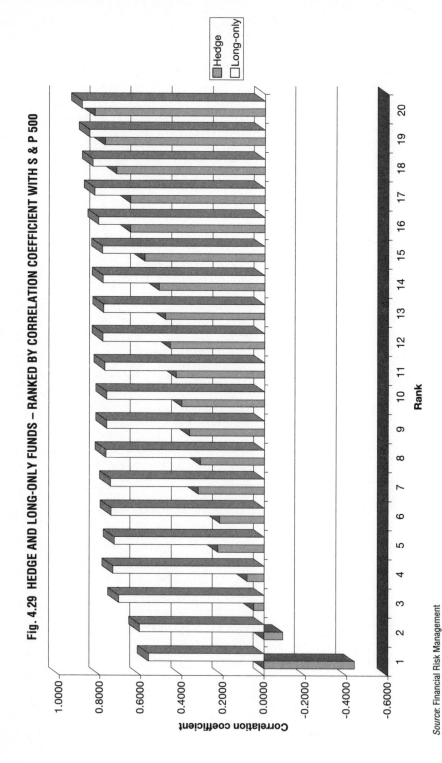

Fig. 4.29 HEDGE AND LONG-ONLY FUNDS – RANKED BY CORRELATION COEFFICIENT WITH S & P 500

Source: Financial Risk Management

THE ACADEMIC STUDY

Another block of research has been conducted over the years by Thomas Schneeweis of the University of Massachusetts. In his "A Comparison of Return Patterns in Traditional and Alternative Investments", Schneeweis looked at monthly returns for a series of commodity, managed futures and hedge fund indices, as well as commonly used stock and bond performance indices for the time period from January 1990 through to December 1995. The indices used included the Standard and Poor's 500 Stock index (S&P 500), the Morgan Stanley Capital International Global Stock index (MSCI), the Salomon Brothers US (US Bond) and World Government Bond index (World Bond), one month Treasury bill yields, the Mt Lucas Commodity Trading index (MLM), the Goldman Sachs Commodity Index (GSCI), JP Morgan Commodity index (JPMCI) and the Producer's Price index. For comparison purposes, Schneeweis used the commodity trading advisor indices from MAR, Tass and Barclay. Because the MAR hedge fund indices began only in May 1994, the reported correlation patterns, tracking error and efficient frontier comparisons were based on monthly data from May 1994 through 1995. Schneeweis reports that the results on the hedge fund indices with data from 1990 to 1995 were also compared and the results were similar.

Looking specifically at the commodity indices, managed futures and hedge fund indices as stand-alone investments, Schneeweis found that for the 1990 to 1995 period, the mean monthly returns of three of the broad-based CTA indices, as well as the traditional financial benchmarks, generally underperformed the reported hedge fund indices (see Figures 4.30 and 4.31).

The results also showed that the monthly standard deviation of the CTA and traditional indices was in each case greater than or similar to most of the hedge fund indices.

Fig. 4.30 HEDGE FUND, CTA AND BENCHMARK INDICES 1990–1995

	January 1990 to December 1996					January 1994 to December 1995				
	Average return	Standard deviation	vg/StDe	Maximum return	Minimum return	Average return	Standard deviation	vg/StDe	Maximum return	Minimum return
MAR CTA Indices										
Dollar–Weight	1.18%	3.40%	0.35	14.47%	-6.00%	0.90%	2.77%	0.32	8.19%	-3.14%
Equal Weight	0.83%	2.97%	0.28	11.28%	-5.43%	0.77%	2.10%	0.37	5.76%	-3.04%
Currency	1.21%	4.95%	0.24	16.36%	-8.17%	0.56%	3.31%	0.17	10.52%	-3.40%
Discretionary	1.27%	2.42%	0.53	8.67%	-4.57%	0.86%	1.50%	0.58	3.49%	-1.00%
Diversified	0.93%	3.78%	0.25	12.69%	-7.53%	1.31%	3.67%	0.36	8.35%	-4.23%
Energy	0.66%	3.15%	0.21	10.02%	-6.11%	0.47%	2.15%	0.22	4.67%	-4.66%
Financial	1.20%	4.15%	0.29	20.17%	-8.56%	0.62%	2.89%	0.22	8.75%	-3.08%
Stock						-0.52%	3.67%	-0.14	7.34%	-7.06%
Trend Following	1.16%	5.40%	0.21	22.03%	-10.38%	0.96%	4.06%	0.24	11.89%	-4.84%
Barclay CTA Indices										
CTA	0.62%	2.86%	0.22	10.03%	-5.49%	0.74%	2.15%	0.35	6.32%	-3.11%
Currency	1.04%	4.55%	0.23	15.00%	-7.67%	0.52%	2.66%	0.19	7.42%	-3.31%
Agricultural	0.68%	2.00%	0.34	5.80%	-4.83%	1.26%	1.71%	0.74	4.99%	-1.68%
Financial/Metal	0.67%	2.45%	0.27	7.05%	-10.19%	-0.04%	3.18%	-0.01	6.31%	-10.19%
Energy	0.80%	3.70%	0.22	26.90%	-4.38%	0.23%	1.85%	0.12	4.46%	-3.39%
Diversified	0.96%	3.73%	0.26	12.03%	-6.61%	1.04%	2.80%	0.37	7.09%	-4.10%
Systematic	0.98%	3.95%	0.25	14.50%	-7.59%	0.86%	2.48%	0.34	7.19%	-3.79%
Discretionary	0.54%	1.53%	0.35	8.47%	-3.01%	0.37%	0.97%	0.38	2.13%	-1.88%
Tass Index	0.72%	3.61%	0.20	15.70%	-7.59%	0.44%	2.44%	0.18	6.19%	-3.09%
Hedge Fund Research Indices										
Convertible Arbitrage	1.10%	1.27%	0.87	4.27%	-2.36%	0.93%	0.96%	0.97	2.31%	-1.13%
Distressed Securities	1.70%	2.15%	0.79	7.33%	-5.53%	1.06%	1.10%	0.96	2.66%	-1.70%
Emerging Markets	2.59%	5.30%	0.49	22.33%	-8.82%	0.45%	3.61%	0.12	9.80%	-5.09%
Fixed Income	1.59%	2.03%	0.79	12.03%	-1.29%	0.68%	0.73%	0.93	2.24%	-0.79%
Foreign Exchange	1.54%	4.59%	0.34	14.63%	-8.19%	1.06%	2.95%	0.36	9.51%	-1.89%
Fund of Funds	1.14%	1.33%	0.86	5.09%	-1.93%	0.68%	1.01%	0.68	2.51%	-1.01%
Growth	1.66%	2.56%	0.65	8.18%	-5.32%	1.58%	2.05%	0.77	6.08%	-1.97%
Macro	2.33%	2.78%	0.84	10.20%	-5.96%	2.13%	2.23%	0.96	7.33%	-1.47%
Market Neutral	1.14%	0.89%	1.28	3.50%	-0.68%	0.89%	0.52%	1.72	1.66%	-0.43%
Market Timing	1.34%	1.90%	0.71	8.92%	-2.50%	1.05%	1.27%	0.82	3.27%	-1.93%
Merger Arbitrage	1.00%	1.46%	0.68	4.17%	-5.40%	0.97%	0.82%	1.19	2.50%	-0.39%
Sector	1.74%	2.38%	0.73	7.56%	-4.62%	1.20%	2.09%	0.58	3.98%	-3.22%
Multi–Strategy	0.92%	1.03%	0.90	2.90%	-1.76%	0.72%	0.98%	0.73	2.23%	-1.26%
Opportunistic	1.86%	2.02%	0.92	8.18%	-2.34%	1.57%	1.67%	0.94	4.33%	-2.34%
Short Selling	0.65%	4.53%	0.14	12.11%	-10.82%	-0.29%	4.80%	-0.06	12.11%	-8.78%
Value	1.67%	1.93%	0.87	6.33%	-4.53%	1.30%	1.49%	0.88	3.63%	-1.96%

MAR Hedge Fund Indices										
Event						0.83%	0.67%	1.24	1.78%	−0.51%
Global						0.11%	1.28%	0.09	2.24%	−2.70%
Macro						0.37%	0.96%	0.38	2.71%	−1.87%
Market Neutral						0.61%	0.38%	1.61	1.24%	0.04%
Short						−0.37%	2.40%	−0.15	3.26%	−4.80%
Opportunistic						0.80%	1.29%	0.62	3.20%	−2.11%
Fund of Funds						0.40%	0.80%	0.50	1.68%	−1.10%
Evaluation Associates (EACM) Indices										
EACM 100	1.33%	0.98%	1.35	4.83%	−0.91%	0.99%	0.88%	1.13	2.37%	−0.34%
Relative Value	0.97%	0.66%	1.48	2.54%	−1.10%	0.78%	0.64%	1.23	1.57%	−0.44%
Long/Short Equity	0.97%	0.89%	1.09	3.51%	−1.04%	0.76%	0.63%	1.20	1.72%	−0.50%
Convertible	0.81%	1.45%	0.56	5.03%	−4.96%	0.77%	1.43%	0.54	2.28%	−3.41%
Bond	0.85%	0.43%	1.98	2.02%	−0.19%	0.82%	0.33%	2.47	1.51%	0.26%
Rotational	1.24%	1.46%	0.85	4.32%	−2.04%	0.79%	0.79%	0.99	2.22%	−0.50%
Event	1.15%	1.54%	0.75	5.08%	−4.75%	1.14%	0.93%	1.22	2.42%	−0.91%
Arbitrage	0.74%	2.13%	0.35	5.90%	−11.10%	0.99%	0.96%	1.04	2.83%	−0.77%
Bankruptcy	1.54%	2.10%	0.73	10.09%	−6.36%	1.25%	1.11%	1.13	2.89%	−0.67%
Multi-Strategy	1.16%	1.32%	0.88	3.69%	−2.66%	1.17%	1.13%	1.03	2.66%	−1.36%
Equity EQ	1.56%	1.86%	0.84	5.37%	−3.40%	1.28%	1.51%	0.85	3.29%	−1.88%
Domestic Long	1.52%	2.41%	0.63	6.67%	−4.64%	1.75%	1.95%	0.90	4.50%	−2.78%
Domestic Opportunity	1.39%	2.04%	0.68	6.66%	−3.00%	1.28%	1.99%	0.64	4.42%	−3.00%
Global	1.76%	3.01%	0.58	8.42%	−8.47%	0.80%	1.91%	0.42	4.37%	−2.18%
Global AA	2.00%	3.50%	0.57	16.59%	−5.37%	1.33%	2.61%	0.51	7.40%	−2.83%
Discretionary	1.70%	2.43%	0.70	7.52%	−5.19%	1.03%	2.03%	0.51	7.52%	−1.51%
Systematic	2.29%	6.13%	0.37	30.32%	−9.98%	1.64%	4.43%	0.37	13.53%	−4.55%
Short	−0.09%	5.71%	−0.02	12.73%	−12.99%	−1.24%	5.61%	−0.22	10.41%	−12.68%
Performance Benchmarks										
MLM Index	0.65%	1.50%	0.43	4.69%	−4.04%	1.15%	1.21%	0.95	3.53%	−0.86%
JP Morgan Commodity	0.47%	4.90%	0.10	20.73%	−13.52%	12.26%	3.29%	0.38	7.87%	−5.73%
GSCI	0.58%.	4.69%	0.12	22.94%	−9.39%	0.89%	3.33%	0.27	10.23%	−6.74%
S&P 500	1.08%	3.42%	0.32	11.47%	−9.16%	1.83%	2.39%	0.76	4.31%	−3.72%
Salomon US Govt. Bond	0.75%	1.27%	0.59	4.07%	−2.31%	0.87%	1.18%	0.74	4.07%	−1.38%
MSCI World Equity	0.64%	4.06%	0.16	10.55%	−10.53%	1.09%	2.58%	0.42	5.02%	−4.32%
Salomon World Govt. Bond	0.90%	1.82%	0.50	5.94%	−3.63%	1.00%	1.87%	0.54	5.94%	−3.44%
US Producer Prices	0.16%	0.40%	0.40	1.90%	−0.80%	0.17%	0.27%	0.64	0.64%	−0.40%
US T-Bill Yield	0.40%	0.13%	3.04	0.66%	0.20%	0.42%	0.06%	6.97	0.50%	0.30%

Source: "A comparison of return patterns in traditional and alternative investments" Thomas Schneeweis

Fig. 4.31 MONTHLY RISK/RETURN PERFORMANCE OF CTA AND HEDGE FUND INDICES, MAY 1990 TO DECEMBER 1995

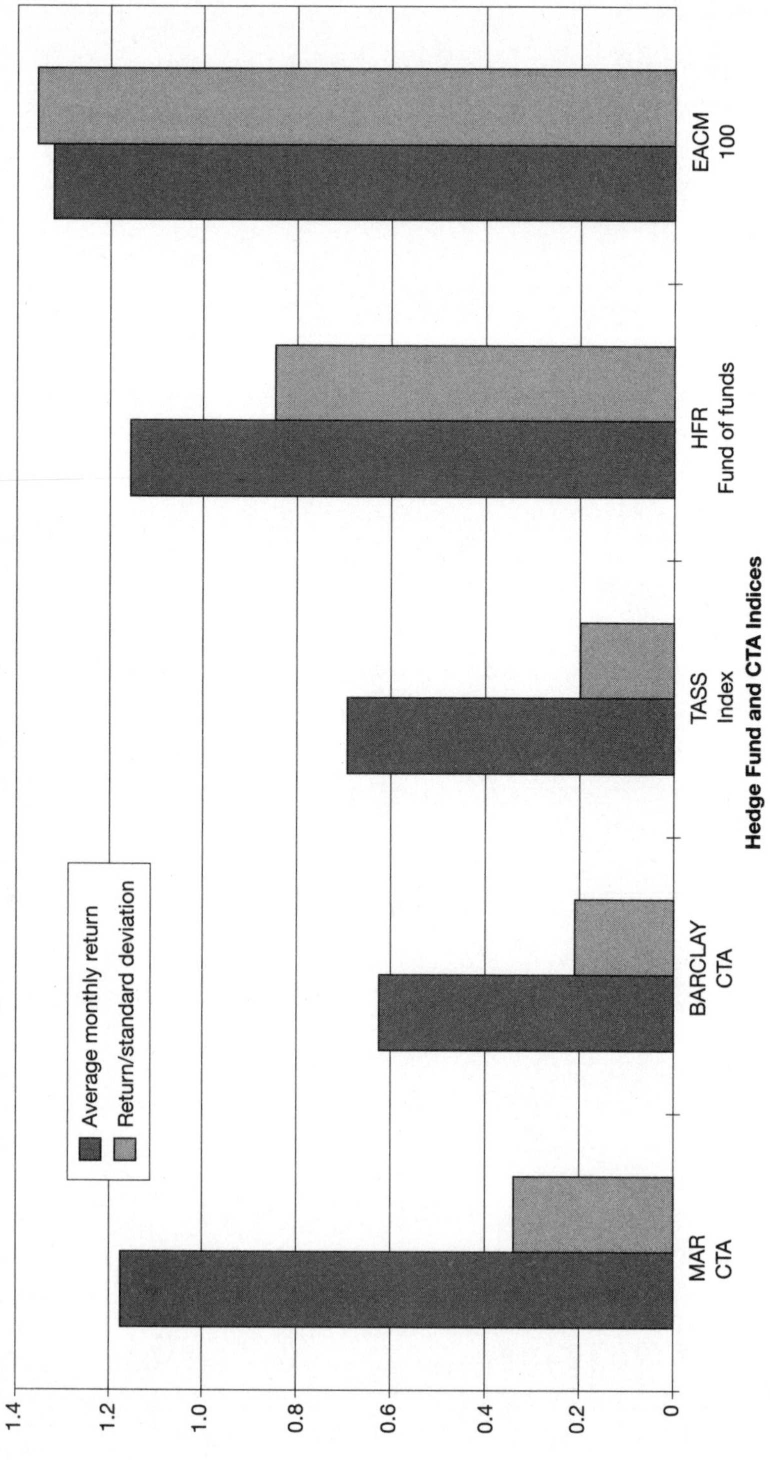

Source: A comparison of return patterns in traditional and alternative investments

Schneeweis says:

> For the period analyzed, the hedge fund index performance represented the most attractive stand-alone risk and return relationship as compared to managed futures indices, commodity indices and other cash market (e.g, stock and bond) indices.

Figures 4.32 to 4.34 illustrate this point and show the average correlation between the CTA indices and sub-indices and the hedge fund indices.

(It is important to point out that the results in this study are conducted at the index level. Research has pointed out that the correlation patterns between individual CTAs or individual hedge funds and traditional asset vehicles may be less consistent than between portfolios of CTAs and hedge funds and traditional asset classes (Henker *et al.*, 1998). Investors must realize that to the degree to which their alternative asset portfolio differs in return performance from that of the comparable alternative asset class index, then asset allocation decisions using index based data may not be reflected in their own performance.)

> "The relatively low average correlations between hedge funds and other asset classes may hide certain simple correlation patterns, claims Schneeweis."

The relatively low average correlations between hedge funds and other asset classes may hide certain simple correlation patterns, claims Schneeweis, and this can be seen in Figures 4.35 and 4.36.

> For instance, the MAR and Barclay systematic or trend following CTA indices are highly correlated (approximately .90) with the EACM Global AA and Systematic indices. This is not unexpected since the EACM Global AA and systematic indices contain a portion of CTA and hedge fund advisors who attempt to capture returns due to trend following or systematic systems ... Lastly, traditional asset classes are also highly correlated with individual hedge fund styles. For instance, the S&P 500 has a positive correlation of over .70 with EACM Domestic Long and negative correlation of over –.70 with EACM Short and HFR Short selling. Thus the usefulness of individual hedge fund indices or sub-indices in portfolio management may be dependent on the individual hedge fund series. Of importance, therefore, is the degree to which a choice of particular hedge fund performance index may impact on an investor's view of hedge fund performance.

Fig. 4.32 CORRELATION BETWEEN MAJOR HEDGE FUND INDICES AND CTA INDICES

	MAR CTA Indices								
	$–Weight	q–Weight	Currency	Discretio	Divers.	Energy	Financial	Stock	Trend
Hedge Fund Research Indices									
Convertible Arbitrage	0.10	−0.06	0.08	0.11	−0.10	0.06	0.18	−0.64	0.07
Distressed Securities	−0.04	−0.10	0.15	0.07	−0.19	0.01	0.14	−0.46	0.04
Emerging Markets	−0.24	−0.29	−0.29	0.18	−0.16	−0.12	−0.24	−0.45	−0.22
Fixed Income	0.58	0.49	0.20	0.20	0.50	0.21	0.66	−0.17	0.56
Foreign Exchange	0.64	0.60	0.93	0.32	0.35	0.10	0.78	0.01	0.63
Fund of Funds	0.32	0.33	0.26	0.60	0.25	0.14	0.41	−0.27	0.32
Growth	−0.17	−0.20	0.08	−0.06	−0.28	−0.15	−0.01	−0.58	−0.10
Macro	0.27	0.32	0.12	0.46	0.21	−0.07	0.37	−0.21	0.27
Market Neutral	0.03	0.06	0.41	−0.08	−0.16	0.03	0.16	−0.35	0.09
Market Timing	−0.14	−0.19	0.00	0.05	−0.22	−0.34	0.00	−0.55	−0.05
Merger Arbitrage	−0.13	−0.22	0.05	−0.03	0.22	0.28	0.02	0.57	−0.07
Sector	0.13	0.08	0.23	0.26	0.03	0.01	0.24	−0.53	0.19
Multi–Strategy	0.17	0.18	0.24	0.42	0.06	0.17	0.31	−0.45	0.21
Opportunistic	0.03	−0.01	0.02	0.14	−0.07	0.14	0.20	−0.32	0.07
Short Selling	0.45	0.47	0.23	0.32	0.47	0.39	0.32	0.66	0.35
Value	0.15	0.09	0.24	0.14	0.03	0.06	0.31	−0.60	0.22
MAR Hedge Fund Indices									
Event	−0.05	−0.10	0.02	0.08	−0.12	0.16	0.04	−0.22	0.00
Global	0.21	0.20	0.23	0.32	0.13	0.15	0.29	−0.51	0.25
Macro	−0.29	−0.30	−0.18	0.07	−0.37	−0.23	−0.07	−0.36	−0.29
Market Neutral	0.20	0.21	0.26	0.28	0.05	0.32	0.35	−0.37	0.21
Short	0.44	0.52	0.07	0.39	0.54	0.31	0.26	0.55	0.39
Opportunistic	−0.34	−0.36	−0.04	−0.21	−0.45	−0.40	−0.15	−0.63	−0.25
Fund of Funds	0.02	0.01	0.01	0.41	−0.02	0.07	0.14	−0.53	0.05
Evaluation Associates (EACM) Indices									
EACM 100	0.66	0.66	0.55	0.64	0.54	0.30	0.67	−0.08	0.67
Relative Value	0.11	0.09	0.33	0.01	−0.08	0.07	0.28	−0.46	0.19
Long/Short Equity	0.07	0.14	0.47	−0.07	−0.10	−0.09	0.15	−0.30	0.15
Convertible	0.12	0.08	0.22	0.13	−0.02	0.02	0.26	−0.48	0.18
Bond	0.21	0.09	0.30	−0.29	0.07	0.19	0.35	−0.23	0.27
Rotational	−0.01	−0.01	0.18	−0.04	−0.15	0.19	0.16	−0.27	0.04
Event	−0.10	−0.16	−0.01	0.14	−0.14	−0.12	0.01	−0.43	−0.05
Arbitrage	−0.28	−0.34	−0.24	0.14	−0.25	−0.27	−0.21	−0.31	−0.26
Bankruptcy	0.09	0.06	0.17	0.11	0.03	0.05	0.16	−0.43	0.15
Multi-Strategy	−0.09	−0.17	0.00	0.11	−0.16	−0.12	0.04	−0.39	−0.05
Equal EQ	−0.09	−0.08	0.00	0.28	−0.13	0.05	−0.01	−0.39	−0.04
Domestic Long	−0.07	−0.09	−0.03	0.14	−0.12	−0.07	0.04	−0.45	−0.01
Domestic Opportunity	0.09	0.16	0.20	0.25	0.02	0.19	0.13	−0.13	0.12
Global	−0.24	−0.26	−0.18	0.25	−0.21	−0.01	−0.21	−0.33	−0.23
Global AA	0.94	0.93	0.69	0.61	0.84	0.26	0.87	0.11	0.93
Discretionary	0.33	0.42	0.33	0.65	0.22	0.16	0.41	0.11	0.32
Systematic	0.95	0.91	0.66	0.43	0.89	0.23	0.84	0.08	0.94
Short	0.44	0.49	0.20	0.34	0.47	0.40	0.30	0.70	0.34
Average	0.13	0.11	0.18	0.20	0.05	0.05	0.22	−0.27	0.16

Source: A comparison of return patterns in traditional and alternative investments

				Barclay CTA Indices					
CTA	Currency	Agric.	Fin/Metal	Energy	Divers.	System.	Discretio	TASS	Average
−0.04	0.05	0.26	−0.11	−0.14	−0.08	0.01	−0.15	−0.04	−0.03
−0.06	0.17	0.09	−0.11	−0.25	−0.16	0.00	−0.23	−0.11	−0.06
−0.28	−0.23	0.29	−0.23	−0.14	−0.25	−0.33	−0.06	−0.22	−0.18
0.51	0.13	0.13	0.28	0.30	0.43	0.45	0.49	0.63	0.36
0.59	0.93	−0.37	0.46	0.08	0.44	0.72	0.35	0.56	0.45
0.25	0.38	0.25	0.10	0.17	0.26	0.34	0.37	0.34	0.27
−0.17	0.13	−0.09	−0.35	−0.34	−0.25	−0.13	−0.35	−0.22	−0.18
0.18	0.26	0.17	0.12	0.06	0.28	0.32	0.37	0.26	0.21
0.01	0.41	−0.21	0.08	−0.08	−0.06	0.12	−0.37	0.01	0.01
−0.14	0.00	0.06	−0.27	−0.40	−0.26	−0.14	−0.25	−0.18	−0.17
−0.19	0.14	0.06	−0.29	−0.28	−0.24	−0.13	−0.24	−0.20	−0.16
0.09	0.32	0.10	−0.06	−0.21	0.05	0.14	0.03	0.09	0.07
0.13	0.29	0.19	−0.01	0.11	0.10	0.23	0.09	0.16	0.14
−0.02	0.13	0.24	−0.06	−0.11	−0.05	0.07	−0.07	−0.02	0.02
0.43	0.18	0.05	0.46	0.56	0.43	0.43	0.52	0.49	0.40
0.10	0.36	−0.02	0.04	−0.14	0.04	0.16	−0.02	0.10	0.07
−0.03	−0.03	0.31	−0.06	−0.08	−0.09	−0.01	−0.23	−0.13	−0.03
0.19	0.23	0.17	−0.02	−0.10	0.16	0.21	0.14	0.21	0.14
−0.31	−0.09	0.07	−0.49	−0.20	−0.29	−0.29	−0.03	−0.29	−0.22
0.16	0.26	0.06	0.01	0.30	0.09	0.25	0.19	0.18	0.17
0.51	0.00	0.09	0.49	0.35	0.57	0.45	0.53	0.46	0.39
−0.39	0.06	−0.25	−0.33	−0.36	−0.44	−0.33	−0.50	−0.36	−0.32
−0.04	0.13	0.30	−0.11	0.07	−0.01	0.02	0.16	0.03	0.04
0.61	0.57	0.13	0.50	0.19	0.58	0.71	0.45	0.62	0.50
0.05	0.29	0.00	0.09	−0.04	−0.03	0.17	−0.14	0.05	0.05
0.11	0.37	−0.26	0.03	−0.19	0.01	0.20	−0.19	0.03	0.03
0.04	0.15	0.09	0.14	0.01	−0.01	0.12	−0.13	0.06	0.05
0.12	0.31	0.02	0.11	−0.01	−0.01	0.17	−0.15	0.20	0.09
−0.05	0.22	0.05	−0.05	0.01	−0.08	0.08	−0.03	−0.06	0.01
−0.10	0.03	0.16	−0.21	−0.19	−0.16	−0.09	−0.26	−0.15	−0.10
−0.31	−0.16	0.37	−0.32	−0.26	−0.28	−0.26	−0.21	−0.34	−0.21
0.12	0.17	−0.04	−0.11	−0.14	0.04	0.09	−0.19	0.07	0.02
−0.12	0.05	0.13	−0.14	−0.11	−0.20	−0.10	−0.27	−0.15	−0.10
−0.11	0.11	0.19	−0.18	−0.15	−0.11	−0.04	−0.10	−0.11	−0.05
−0.10	0.10	0.14	−0.09	−0.29	−0.11	−0.02	−0.26	−0.12	−0.08
0.09	0.27	0.08	−0.04	−0.04	0.11	0.20	0.01	0.08	0.10
−0.26	−0.13	0.22	−0.29	−0.03	−0.26	−0.28	0.03	−0.22	−0.15
0.92	0.63	0.00	0.75	0.23	0.87	0.95	0.65	0.90	0.67
0.29	0.49	0.08	0.32	0.26	0.33	0.44	0.58	0.30	0.34
0.95	0.52	−0.04	0.73	0.15	0.88	0.92	0.50	0.92	0.64
0.42	0.24	0.03	0.51	0.55	0.47	0.45	0.58	0.48	0.41
0.10	0.21	0.08	0.03	−0.02	0.07	0.15	0.04	0.10	

Fig. 4.33 CORRELATION BETWEEN MAJOR HEDGE FUND INDICES

	CA	DS	EM	FI	FX	FOF	GR	MA	MN	MT	AR	SEC	MS	OP	SHT	VAL
						HFR Hedge Fund Indices										
Hedge Fund Research Indices																
Convertible Arbitrage		.78	.47	.22	.15	.59	.75	.48	.40	.58	.69	.76	.74	.73	−.58	.73
Distressed Securities	.78		.34	.04	.16	.53	.84	.30	.39	.71	.70	.80	.74	.86	−.64	.78
Emerging Markets	.47	.34		−.02	−.23	.52	.39	.20	−.07	.43	.45	.60	.23	.21	−.41	.50
Fixed Income	.22	.04	−.02		.29	.33	−.07	.29	−.06	.12	−.03	.14	.30	.13	.23	.18
Foreign Exchange	.15	.16	−.23	.29		.40	.13	.27	.32	.00	.16	.31	.32	.16	.22	.36
Fund of Funds	.59	.53	.52	.33	.40		.53	.77	.22	.36	.51	.80	.77	.60	−.17	.67
Growth	.75	.84	.39	−.07	.13	.53		.37	.38	.74	.82	.82	.67	.77	−.83	.79
Macro	.48	.30	.20	.29	.27	.77	.37		.05	.22	.43	.51	.58	.58	−.14	.41
Market Neutral	.40	.39	−.07	−.06	.32	.22	.38	.05		.11	.14	.28	.45	.20	−.23	.35
Market Timing	.58	.71	.43	.12	.00	.36	.74	.22	.11		.64	.65	.52	.61	−.68	.60
Merger Arbitrage	.69	.70	.45	−.03	.16	.51	.82	.43	.14	.64		.74	.47	.73	−.68	.78
Sector	.76	.80	.60	.14	.31	.80	.82	.51	.28	.65	.74		.78	.75	−.62	.91
Multi-Strategy	.74	.74	.23	.30	.32	.77	.67	.58	.45	.52	.47	.78		.76	−.37	.67
Opportunistic	.73	.86	.21	.13	.16	.60	.77	.58	.20	.61	.73	.75	.76		−.53	.75
Short Selling	−.58	−.64	−.41	.23	.22	−.17	−.83	−.14	−.23	−.68	−.68	−.62	−.37	−.53		−.60
Value	.73	.78	.50	.18	.36	.67	.79	.41	.35	.60	.78	.91	.67	.75	−.60	
MAR Hedge Fund Indices																
Event	.66	.78	.13	−.10	.02	.27	.59	.11	.22	.41	.56	.45	.47	.69	−.42	.46
Global	.70	.59	.59	.33	.25	.81	.59	.51	.46	.41	.42	.78	.70	.49	−.32	.70
Macro	.48	.51	.32	.01	−.11	.45	.67	.57	.03	.52	.56	.53	.43	.57	−.67	.43
Market Neutral	.63	.45	.05	.45	.38	.57	.37	.49	.49	.16	.25	.40	.73	.49	.01	.42
Short	−.53	−.37	−.46	.10	−.05	−.21	−.65	−.09	−.30	−.54	−.68	−.50	−.26	−.33	.68	−.51
Opportunistic	.61	.74	.45	−.17	−.05	.36	.84	.25	.44	.62	.70	.67	.49	.56	−.85	.67
Fund of Funds	.71	.67	.67	.23	.14	.89	.65	.63	.28	.45	.64	.84	.75	.67	−.42	.78
Evaluation Associates (EACM) Indices																
EACM 100	.48	.47	.18	.39	.63	.82	.31	.61	.24	.17	.27	.61	.69	.52	.13	.53
Relative Value	.76	.65	.11	.19	.32	.40	.45	.32	.67	.24	.40	.45	.63	.51	−.21	.49
Long/Short Equity	.19	.22	−.24	.08	.34	.07	.17	−.05	.81	.08	−.08	.08	.33	−.01	−.04	.11
Convertible	.83	.60	.30	.19	.22	.43	.42	.38	.47	.29	.42	.45	.57	.47	−.22	.45
Bond	.54	.54	.15	.30	.32	.24	.34	.02	.43	.26	.48	.41	.31	.43	−.15	.54
Rotational	.55	.62	−.08	.09	.23	.34	.39	.36	.47	.07	.39	.39	.60	.63	−.19	.44
Event	.67	.76	.47	−.10	.05	.50	.84	.31	.09	.71	.87	.71	.48	.73	−.67	.70
Arbitrage	.42	.49	.42	−.17	−.09	.41	.60	.39	−.21	.52	.82	.50	.28	.63	−.53	.47
Bankruptcy	.67	.77	.42	−.03	.11	.49	.84	.19	.35	.66	.63	.74	.55	.60	−.63	.72
Multi-Strategy	.65	.70	.39	−.07	.10	.41	.76	.25	.05	.67	.83	.61	.42	.68	−.59	.64
Equity EQ	.69	.77	.60	−.03	.11	.80	.82	.52	.25	.58	.65	.89	.78	.75	−.58	.74
Domestic Long	.67	.80	.43	−.05	.10	.63	.87	.51	.21	.69	.81	.82	.66	.89	−.68	.81
Domestic Opportunity	47	.54	.08	.03	.30	.63	.61	.48	.33	.27	.32	.65	.78	.61	−.35	.45
Global	.46	.46	.91	−.05	−.16	.59	.42	.21	.04	.39	.38	.59	.35	.25	−.31	.45
Global AA	.09	.02	−.16	.56	.71	.47	−.13	.40	.04	−.09	−.11	.21	.31	.10	.47	.19
Discretionary	.22	.29	.05	.14	.47	.67	.11	.71	.03	.00	.12	.38	.52	.42	.19	.28
Systematic	.00	−.11	−.21	.60	.62	.25	−.20	.14	03	−.11	−.19	.07	.13	−.08	.47	.09
Short	−.61	−.63	−.42	.13	.23	−.12	−.83	−.03	−.23	−.75	−.68	−.57	−.35	−.48	.96	−.55
Average	.48	.48	.24	.15	.22	.48	.44	.35	.23	.32	.40	.50	.49	.47	−.24	.47

Source: A comparison of return patterns in traditional and alternative investments

	MAR Hedge Fund Indices						EACM Hedge Fund Indices																	
EV	GL	MA	MN	SHT	OP	FOF	100	RV	LS	CO	BH	RO	EV	AR	BK	MS	EQ	LO	OP	GL	AA	DIS	SYS	SHT
.66	.70	.48	.63	−.53	.61	.71	.48	.76	.19	.83	.54	.55	.67	.42	.67	.65	.69	.67	.47	.46	.09	.22	.00	−.61
.78	.59	.51	.45	−.37	.74	.67	.47	.65	.22	.60	.54	.62	.76	.49	.77	.70	.77	.80	.54	.46	.02	.29	−.11	−.63
.13	.59	.32	.05	−.46	.45	.67	.18	.11	−.24	.30	.15	−.08	.47	.42	.42	.39	.60	.43	.08	.91	−.16	.05	−.21	−.42
.10	.33	.01	.45	.10	−.17	.23	.39	.19	.08	.19	.30	.09	−.10	−.17	−.03	−.07	−.03	−.05	.03	−.05	.56	.14	.60	.13
.02	.25	−.11	.38	−.05	−.05	.14	.63	.32	.34	.22	.32	.23	.05	−.09	.11	.10	.11	.10	.30	−.16	.71	.47	.62	.23
.27	.81	.45	.57	−.21	.36	.89	.82	.40	.07	.43	.24	.34	.50	.41	.49	.41	.80	.63	.63	.59	.47	.67	.25	−.12
.59	.59	.67	.37	−.65	.84	.65	.31	.45	.17	.42	.34	.39	.84	.60	.84	.76	.82	.87	.61	.42	−.13	.11	−.20	−.83
.11	.51	.57	.49	−.09	.25	.63	.61	.32	−.05	.38	.02	.36	.31	.39	.19	.25	.52	.51	.48	.21	.40	.71	.14	−.03
.22	.46	.03	.49	−.30	.44	.28	.24	.67	.81	.47	.43	.47	.09	−.21	.35	.05	.25	.21	.33	.04	.04	.03	.03	−.23
.41	.41	.52	.16	−.54	.62	.45	.17	.24	.08	.29	.26	.07	.71	.52	.66	.67	.58	.69	.27	.39	−.09	.00	−.11	−.75
.56	.42	.56	.25	−.68	.70	.64	.27	.40	−.08	.42	.48	.39	.87	.82	.63	.83	.65	.81	.32	.38	−.11	.12	−.19	−.68
.45	.78	.53	.40	−.50	.67	.84	.61	.45	.08	.45	.41	.39	.71	.50	.74	.61	.89	.82	.65	.59	.21	.38	.07	−.57
.47	.70	.45	.73	−.26	.49	.75	.69	.63	.33	.57	.31	.60	.48	.28	.55	.42	.78	.66	.78	.35	.31	.52	.13	−.35
.69	.49	.57	.49	−.33	.56	.67	.52	.51	−.01	.47	.43	.63	.73	.63	.60	.68	.75	.89	.61	.25	.10	.42	−.08	−.48
.42	−.32	−.67	.01	−.68	−.85	−.42	.13	−.21	−.04	−.22	−.15	−.19	−.67	−.53	−.63	−.59	−.58	−.68	−.35	−.31	.47	.19	.47	.96
.46	.70	.43	.42	−.51	.67	.78	.53	.49	.11	.45	.54	.44	.70	.47	.72	.64	.74	.81	.45	.45	.19	.28	.09	−.55
	.26	.27	.35	−.16	.39	.41	.37	.56	.09	.58	.43	.51	.74	.53	.64	.77	.53	.58	.41	.24	.00	.21	−.10	−.44
.26		.38	.64	−.29	.45	.85	.65	.57	.38	.54	.36	.42	.40	.18	.57	.26	.73	.54	.48	.68	.32	.36	.22	−.32
.27	.38		.17	−.36	.66	.55	.03	.11	−.14	.16	−.11	.22	.56	.53	.48	.46	.54	.57	.34	.35	−.27	.22	−.42	−.61
.35	.64	.17		−.11	.18	.59	.64	.78	.53	.68	.37	.70	.17	.02	.24	.18	.44	.29	.49	.24	.37	.51	.20	−.02
.16	−.29	−.36	−.11		−.63	−.35	.11	−.24	−.09	−.25	−.39	−.08	−.51.	−.47	−.37	−.51	−.45	−.51	−.23	−.29	.42	.27	.37	.72
.39	.45	.66	.18	−.63		.56	.06	.44	.15	.44	.33	.37	65	.42	.68	.58	.64	.69	.35	.46	−.36	.00	−.42	−.81
.41	.85	.55	.59	−.35	.56		.62	.50	.11	.50	.31	.48	.59	.51	.55	.50	.84	.70	.53	.73	.16	.52	−.04	−.37
.37	.65	.03	.64	.11	.06	.62		.51	.22	.51	.33	.41	.33	.16	.38	.30	.59	.45	.61	.31	.81	.75	.61	.17
.56	.57	.11	.78	−.24	.44	.50	.51		.59	.90	.69	.83	.27	.03	.36	.29	.40	.33	.35	.26	.20	.33	.08	−.23
.09	.38	−.14	.53	−.09	.15	.11	.22	.59		.31	.25	.43	−.16	−.34	.08	−.19	.08	−.05	.26	−.05	.16	.09	.15	−.07
.58	.54	.16	.68	−.25	.44	.50	.51	.90	.31		.58	.60	.38	.11	.43	.43	.42	.34	.26	.38	.21	.31	.10	−.26
.43	.36	−.11	.37	−.39	.33	.31	.33	.69	.25	.58		.54	.31	.08	.36	.35	.22	.30	.06	.16	.14	−.04	.18	−.21
.51	.42	.22	.70	−.08	.37	.48	.41	.83	.43	.60	.54		.18	.14	.17	.15	.38	.36	.41	.12	.07	.44	−.11	−.12
.74	.40	.56	.17	−.51	.65	.59	.33	.27	−.16	.38	.31	.18		.81	.84	.97	.72	.85	.40	.43	−.07	.11	−.13	−.69
.53	.18	.53	.02	−.47	.42	.51	.16	.03	−.34	.11	.08	.14	.82		.40	.78	.59	.75	.29	.33	−.19	.15	−.30	−.52
.64	.57	.48	.24	−.37	.68	.55	.38	.36	.08	.43	.36	.17	.84	.40		.76	.68	.71	.42	.46	.05	.04	.04	−.67
.77	.26	.46	.18	−.51	.58	.50	.30	.29	−.19	.43	.35	.15	.97	.78	.76		.62	.77	.32	.34	−.06	.11	−.12	−.63
.53	.73	.54	.44	−.45	.64	.84	.59	.40	.08	.42	.22	.38	.72	.59	.68	.62		.86	.79	.68	.07	.45	−.12	−.53
.58	.54	.57	.29	−.51	.69	.70	.45	.33	−.05	.34	.30	.36	.85	.75	.71	.77	.86		.60	.38	.01	.27	−.12.	−.63
.41	.48	.34	.49	−.23	.35	.53	.61	.35	.26	.26	.06	.41	.40	.29	.42	.32	.79	.60		.20	.25	.51	06	−27
.24	.68	.35	.24	−.29	.46	.73	.31	.26	−.05	.38	.16	.12	.43	.33	.46	.34	.68	.38	.20		−.11	.25	−.24	−.32
.00	.32	−.27	.37	.42	−.36	.16	.81	.20	.16	.21	.14	.07	−.07	−.19	.05	−.06	.07	.01	.25	−.11		.55	.92	.47
.21	.36	.22	.51	.27	.00	.52	.75	.33	.09	.31	−.04	.44	.11	.15	.04	.11	.45	.27	.51	.25	.55		.19	.33
.10	.22	−.42	.20	.37	−.42	−.04	.61	.08	.15	.10	.18	−.11	−.13	−.30	.04	−.12	−.12	−.12	.06	−.24	.92	.19		.40
.44	−.32	−.61	−.02	.72	−.81	−.37	.17	−.23	−.07	−.26	−.21	−.12	−.69	−.52	−.67	−.63	−.53	−.63	−.27	−.32	.47	.33	.40	
.35	.46	.27	.39	−.20	.33	.49	.44	.40	.14	.39	.29	.34	.40	.27	.40	.36	.48	.44	.37	.29	.20	.31	.10	−.23

117

Fig. 4.34 CORRELATION BETWEEN MAJOR HEDGE FUND INDICES AND PERFORMANCE BENCHMARKS

	MLM	JPMCI	GSCI	SP500	US BOND	MSCI EQUITY	WORLD BOND	PPI	US TREASURY BILL
Hedge Fund Research Indices									
Convertible Arbitrage	−0.28	−0.05	0.15	0.63	0.42	0.55	0.29	−0.14	0.43
Distressed Securities	−0.35	−0.15	0.14	0.71	0.30	0.56	0.31	−0.21	0.56
Emerging Markets	0.08	−0.19	−0.13	0.26	−0.03	0.31	−0.11	0.12	−0.10
Fixed Income	−0.28	0.34	0.30	0.00	0.30	0.19	0.34	0.04	0.18
Foreign Exchange	−0.37	0.38	0.22	−0.10	−0.14	0.16	0.28	−0.34	0.07
Fund of Funds	−0.12	0.39	0.48	0.21	0.01	0.42	−0.02	0.03	0.26
Growth	−0.41	−0.15	0.08	0.71	0.06	0.70	0.20	−0.10	0.38
Macro	−0.24	0.24	0.34	0.15	0.14	0.18	−0.31	0.15	0.24
Market Neutral	−0.18	−0.01	0.38	0.30	0.28	0.40	0.40	0.03	0.68
Market Timing	−0.41	−0.25	0.01	0.75	0.21	0.69	0.26	−0.24	0.16
Merger Arbitrage	−0.35	−0.23	−0.11	0.58	0.10	0.45	0.00	0.02	0.15
Sector	−0.33	0.09	0.24	0.54	0.07	0.61	0.13	−0.16	0.34
Multi–Strategy	−0.26	0.27	0.48	0.55	0.30	0.61	0.26	−0.15	0.58
Opportunistic	−0.31	0.04	0.29	0.68	0.36	0.50	0.09	−0.11	0.44
Short Selling	0.42	0.46	0.23	−0.69	−0.15	−0.49	−0.04	0.07	−0.36
Value	−0.43	0.05	0.22	0.66	0.27	0.65	0.25	0.03	0.37
MAR Hedge Fund Indices									
Event	0.02	−0.12	0.02	0.50	0.34	0.21	0.37	−0.21	0.36
Global	−0.13	0.21	0.44	0.33	0.12	0.58	0.19	0.11	0.42
Macro	−0.58	−0.06	0.06	0.47	−0.04	0.43	−0.27	−0.02	0.27
Market Neutral	−0.13	0.26	0.45	0.28	0.42	0.37	0.27	0.12	0.52
Short	0.30	0.38	0.20	−0.43	−0.04	−0.42	0.03	0.15	−0.04
Opportunistic	−0.52	−0.44	−0.16	0.66	0.12	0.56	0.09	0.04	0.51
Fund of Funds	−0.14	0.13	0.33	0.44	0.22	0.47	−0.01	0.21	0.41
Evaluation Associates (EACM) Indices									
EACM 100	0.03	0.46	0.47	0.08	0.12	0.26	0.27	−0.09	0.27
Relative Value	−0.18	−0.13	0.17	0.35	0.50	0.25	0.33	−0.02	0.67
Long/Short Equity	−0.06	−0.07	0.29	0.09	0.25	0.19	0.36	0.00	0.62
Convertible	−0.15	−0.16	0.02	0.37	0.49	0.26	0.35	−0.06	0.46
Bond	−0.19	−0.10	0.12	0.22	0.32	0.20	0.34	−0.10	0.31
Rotational	−0.19	−0.05	0.22	0.30	0.41	0.10	0.01	0.07	0.70
Event	−0.21	−0.11	−0.03	−0.66	0.07	0.55	0.23	−0.09	0.08
Arbitrage	−0.01	−0.23	−0.19	0.44	0.00	0.23	−0.19	0.02	−0.07
Bankruptcy	−0.30	0.08	0.21	0.63	0.03	0.72	0.45	−0.10	0.24
Multi–Strategy	−0.22	−0.16	−0.12	0.63	0.16	0.47	0.29	−0.15	0.04
Equity EQ	−0.06	0.02	0.23	0.49	0.04	0.52	0.03	−0.09	0.35
Domestic Long	−0.23	−0.09	0.15	0.72	0.20	0.62	0.10	0.00	0.32
Domestic Opportunity	−0.01	0.25	0.37	0.22	−0.02	0.31	0.06	−0.29	0.44
Global	0.11	−0.11	0.00	0.19	−0.09	0.28	−0.10	0.08	0.05
Global AA	0.00	0.58	0.41	−0.21	0.03	0.05	0.35	−0.10	0.04
Discretionary	−0.05	0.33	0.35	−0.06	0.11	−0.10	−0.23	−0.05	0.25
Systematic	0.02	0.53	0.32	−0.22	−0.02	0.11	0.52	−0.10	−0.07
Short	0.41	0.47	0.26	−0.72	−0.12	−0.58	−0.19	0.12	−0.29
Average	−0.15	0.08	0.19	0.30	0.15	0.32	0.15	−0.04	0.27

Source: "A comparison of return patterns in traditional and alternative investments," Thomas Schneeweis

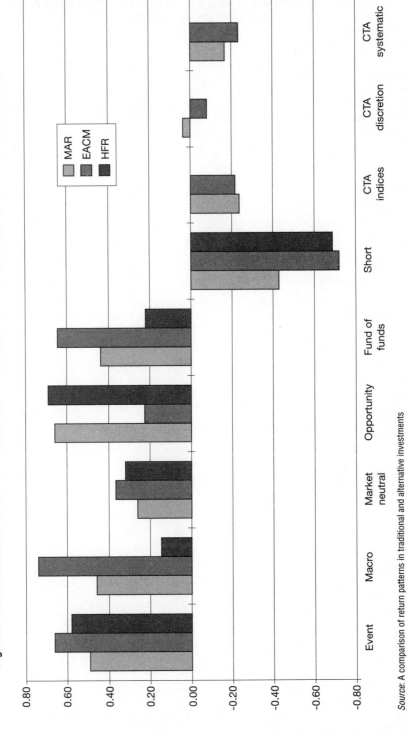

Fig. 4.35 CORRELATION BETWEEN HEDGE FUND AND CTA INDICES WITH SP 500 INDEX, MAY 1994 TO DECEMBER 1995

Source: A comparison of return patterns in traditional and alternative investments

119

Fig. 4.36 CORRELATION BETWEEN HEDGE FUND AND CTA INDICES WITH US BOND INDEX, MAY 1994 TO DECEMBER 1995

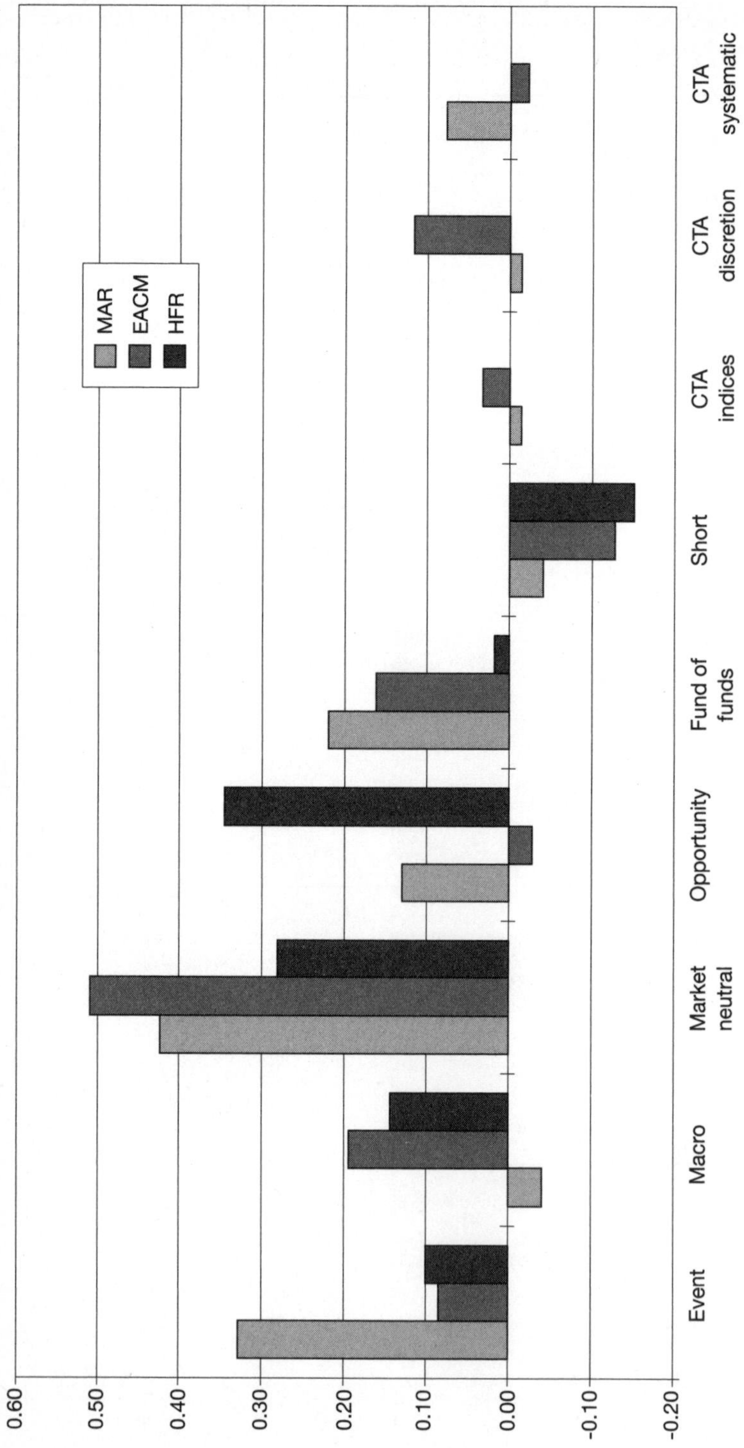

Source: A comparison of return patterns in traditional and alternative investments

Schneeweis's conclusions from his study were that differing correlation exists between various traditional and alternative investment strategies.

More importantly, these correlation patterns reflect the underlying return strategies of these investment vehicles. These results are significant because, if different market factors or investment conditions result in differing mutual fund, hedge fund and CTA return processes, then investors who wish to capture the returns generated by these market factors or trading styles must diversify across alternative as well as traditional investment areas.

PUTTING IT TOGETHER: FUND SELECTION AND RISK ANALYSIS

How to combine all the information and put together a portfolio of hedge funds. Or, how to choose a hedge fund consultant or fund of funds. Here is the Hedge Funds Risk Measurer to help analyze potential investments.

So, you have made it this far: you're blinded by the science and impressed with those statistics and you are still determined to invest in hedge funds. The next stage is choosing hedge funds in which to invest. Here you can either go it alone, or call for help. Help comes in the form of a number of hedge fund or alternative investment management consultants.

FUNDS OF FUNDS

The simplest route to establishing professional help with combining a portfolio of hedge funds is through using a fund of funds. Sohail Jaffer of Citibank writes in *Evaluating and Implementing Hedge Fund Strategies* that there are around 250 funds of funds worldwide accounting for around 20% of total hedge fund assets.

As explained in Chapter 2, the good news about funds of funds is that they can give you the spread of types of investments that you want, without having to put up $1m each time, leaving you to rest in the happy knowledge that a professional manager is managing the hedge fund investments for you, usually on a more sophisticated basis than a private investor could achieve at home. Figure 5.1 ranks hedge funds and funds of funds by assets.

The bad news is that the fund of funds that you choose may perform badly. Even within a top 10 of funds of funds, the performance figures can vary wildly. See Figures 5.2 to 5.5 for some fund of funds rankings.

Also, funds of funds carry an extra level of fees, on top of the management and performance fees of the hedge funds – this was outlined in detail in Chapter 2.

Fig.5.1 HEDGE FUNDS AND FUNDS OF FUNDS BY ASSET SIZE, 1996

The largest hedge funds		The largest fund of funds	
Fund name	Assets ($m)		Assets ($m)
1. Long Term Capital+	9,539.00	1. Haussman Holdings N.V.	3,100.00
2. Jaguar Fund N.V.	5,600.00	2. Permal Investment Holdings N.V. (A)	1,500.00
3. Quantum Fund N.V.	5,454.00	3. IVY Asset Mgt. Corp. Composite	940.00
4. Moore Global Investment+	3,000.00	4. GAM Diversity Fund Inc. (US$)	791.00
5. Quantum Industrial Fund	2,756.20	5. Permal Emerging Markets Holdings (A)	748.20
6. Quota Fund N.V.	2,478.60	6. Common Fund	676.00
7. Kingdon Partners+	2,300.00	7. Blackstone+	508.50
8. Quantum Emerging Growth Fund	1,996.80	8. Meisirow Alternative Strategies Fund	468.80
9. Tiger	1,900.00	9. Garantia Fund of Funds (A)	357.00
10. Quasar Intl. Fund N.V.	1,768.70	10. Permal Millennium Debt Holdings (A)	297.10
11. SBC Currency Portfolio	1,567.00	11. Prima Capital Fund	273.00
12. Cortex	1,431.00	12. Permal Asian Holdings N.V. (A)	264.30
13. Intercap	1,418.00	13. Aurora	247.60
14. Orbis Global Equity	1,091.90	14. Republic Multi-Adviser Arbitrage	236.92
15. Orbis Optimal	1,045.10	15. Man-Glenwood Multi-Strategy Fund	224.66
16. Everest Capital Intl.	1,008.00	16. Mesirow Guardian Fund	213.80
17. Omega Overseas Partners+	1,000.00	17. GSAM Composite Inc.	213.50
18. Hermitage Fund	843.04	18. Garantia Fund of Funds (C)	197.00
19. Zweig Dimenna Special Opport.+	828.00	19. GAM Emerging Markets Multi-Fund Inc.	193.60
20. Puma	825.00	20. Garantia Fund of Funds (B)	188.00

17 hedge funds have over $1 billion in assets; another 20 have assets between $5000m and $999m. Only two funds of funds have over £1bn in assets; another five have assets between $500m and $999m.

+Estimate from secondary sources

Source: MAR/Hedge

Fig. 5.2 FUNDS OF FUNDS RANKINGS: HIGHEST RETURNS, 1996

Fund of funds	Return (%)	Assets Dec–96 ($m)
1. Gems Russia Fund (A)	87.99	7.00
2. Aurum Multi-fund	71.33	n/a
3. RSM	49.86	11.00
4. Sandalwood Select Russia Fund	44.21	2.50
5. Magnum US Equity Fund	42.55	10.00
6. K2 Investment Partners	37.67	29.00
7. Taiwan Arbitrage Co.	34.33	11.30
8. Momentum Stockmaster Fund	33.30	24.35
9. Coast Diversified Fund	30.97	17.10
10. Torrey Global Fund	30.70	62.00

Source: MAR/Hedge

Fig. 5.3 FUNDS OF FUNDS RANKINGS: SMALLEST DECLINE, 1996

Fund of funds	Cumulative decline* (%)	Standard deviation (%)	Assets Dec–96 ($m)
1. Rosewood Associates	0.00	0.86	90.70
2. The Optima Alternative Strat. Fund	0.00	1.03	41.90
3. Oakwood Associates	0.00	1.07	45.00
4. Blue Rock Capital Fund	0.00	1.08	15.35
5. Dillon/Flaherty Market Neutral Fund	0.00	1.18	54.00
6. Ironwood Partners	0.00	1.25	20.13
7. Mesirow Alternative Strategies Fund	0.00	1.29	339.50
8. Ivy Asset Mgt. Corp. Composite	0.00	1.47	617.00
9. Alpha Neutral Fund	0.00	1.60	6.70
10. Momentum Sandalwood Fund	0.00	1.62	10.35

In the case of a tie in lowest cumulative decline, ranking is by lowest standard deviation

Source: MAR/Hedge

Fig. 5.4 FUNDS OF FUNDS RANKINGS: LEAST VOLATILE, 1996

Fund of funds	Standard deviation (%)	Assets Dec–96 ($m)
1. Rosewood Associates	0.86	90.70
2. The Optima Alternative Strat.	1.03	41.90
3. Oakwood Associates	1.07	45.00
4. Blue Rock Capital Fund	1.08	15.35
5. Dillon/Flaherty Mkt. Neutral	1.18	54.00
6. Ironwood Partners	1.25	20.13
7. Mesirow Alternative Strat.	1.29	339.50
8. Ivy Asset Mgt. Corp. Composite	1.47	617.00
9. Alpha Neutral Fund	1.60	6.70
10. Momentum Sandalwood Fund	1.62	10.35

Source: MAR/Hedge

Fig. 5.5 FUNDS OF FUNDS RANKINGS: HIGHEST SHARPE RATIO, 1996

Fund of funds	Sharpe ratio (%)	Assets Dec–96 ($m)
1. Mesirow Alternative Strategies Fund	12.11	339.50
2. Rosewood Associates	10.34	90.70
3. Dillon/Flaherty Market Neutral Fund	9.80	54.00
4. Ironwood Partners	9.25	20.13
5. Oakwood Associates	8.35	45.00
6. Ivy Asset Mgt. Corp. Composite	8.18	617.00
7. The Optima Alternative Strat. Fund	7.89	41.90
8. Blue Rock Capital Fund	7.18	15.35
9. Halcyon Event-Driven Multi Mgr. Fund	6.99	12.97
10. K2 Investment Partners	6.55	29.00

Source: MAR/Hedge

CONSULTANTS

Often the same as fund of funds managers, consultants will act for you in putting together a portfolio of hedge fund investments. You usually need to be a substantial investor to interest a consultant in creating a tailor-made portfolio for you – the type of private investor who is so wealthy that he becomes an institution in his own right.

Lois Peltz of *MAR/Hedge* interviewed Sandra Manzke of US-based consultants Tremont in February 1997 and drew a clear picture of how that consultant works:

Tremont's consulting services consist of advising clients on investment objectives, establishing asset allocation parameters, providing advice in the evaluation and selection of investment managers, custodians and trustees. Tremont recommends structural changes within investment programs such as the addition of new managers or the termination of existing managers. For its consulting clients, Tremont only makes recommendations; each client acts upon these recommendations independently. Compensation for these services varies and is based on the scope of the services provided. Although Tremont does some fixed-fee business, most of its compensation is asset based.

Tremont charges 4% of revenue in soft dollar arrangements and 96% in hard dollar arrangements. Consulting is the core of its business with 50% of its revenue coming from US clients and 30% from international clientele.

London-based independent investment advisory company Financial Risk Management, whose research work is quoted in Chapter 4, identifies funds and fund managers, categorizes them, researches the performance characteristics of the different hedge fund strategy sectors and researches the performance characteristics of the individual hedge fund managers. FRM selects managers and constructs and monitors portfolios on a discretionary or non-discretionary basis for investors. Its fees are negotiable, but it charges roughly 1.0% of assets in management fees for non-discretionary clients and for discretionary clients, a performance fee of 10%. All rebated commissions are refunded to the clients and there are no soft dollar dealings. FRM also offers a fund of funds called Absolute Alpha.

Financial Risk Management
43–44 Albemarle Street
London W1X 3FE
Tel: 171 460 5250   Fax: 171 460 5251

ISSUES IN ASSESSING HEDGE FUNDS

Ed Conco, writing in *Evaluating and Implementing Hedge Fund Strategies*, presented the following list of responsibilities for a hedge fund investor:

- He must determine by himself, with his financial experts, and through discussion with a range of prospective managers, just what kind of financial environment exists.
- He must allocate his resources in some intelligent manner so that his safety, privacy , risk and investment reward are all in some balance, consistent with the environment we are in.
- He must then undertake original due diligence in his search for managers, digging very deep into all aspects of the manager, his organi-

zation, and his methods of investment. Responsibility does not end once a manager has been chosen. The investor must then monitor performance and behaviour closely, constantly weighing what the investment results are, what he has been told, what any regulatory organizations have to report about the manager and so on. This is an endless job. But it is a job that involves the very survival of the investor. The road along which the passive investor travels is lined with the detritus of broken fortunes and lives.

These are stern words but given that hedge funds are largely unregulated, investors do need to be pro-active in managing their investments. Financial Risk Management describes the goal of due diligence as "minimizing surprises" and lists the key topics that need to be evaluated as:

1. People and organization
2. Investment strategy
3. Portfolio construction and risk management
4. Risk controls
5. Performance
6. Investment terms.

> **"Given that hedge funds are largely unregulated, investors do need to be proactive in managing their investments."**

FRM believes that hedge fund managers represent two businesses: the first is the asset selection business and the second is a money management business, with all its additional concerns of portfolio construction and risk management.

THE HEDGE FUNDS RISK MEASURER

The hedge funds risk measurer suggests some areas to investigate in your due diligence research. You must get professional advice beyond this before investing, but these points will give you some ideas.

■ HEDGE FUNDS RISK MEASURER ■

1. Does the hedge fund manager invest his own money in his fund?　　　　　　　　　　　　Yes ☐ No ☐

This is the critical point for most consultants and indeed for hedge fund managers themselves. It's the hedge fund version of "Le Patron mange ici." If their net worth is in the same basket as yours, you're guaranteed a nice, steady investment experience.

2. Is the fund registered by a regulatory body of which you have heard, such as the SEC or the SFA?　　Yes ☐ No ☐

Trust your memory here. You have probably heard of the major regulatory bodies, responsible for protecting investors' assets, without realizing it. While there is still, regrettably, the odd disaster in investment protection, the major financial centres (the US or the UK, for instance) have become a lot wiser and better regulated. Approbation by one of these is a pretty good indicator of probity. However, do be careful that the scheme into which you are entering is covered by investor regulation before contenting yourself that the regulations are thorough. A recent scandal in the UK involved investors simply buying shares in a company which then invested. The investors' position was governed by company law not by investment law and they had no redress.

3. Is the fund located in a financial centre or an offshore centre with which you are familiar and could you point it out on a map?　　　　　　Yes ☐ No ☐

This is a very simple way of telling in the first instance whether the fund is properly regulated. The more obscure a financial centre, the less likely it is to have proper regulation. And don't be blinded by the promise of secrecy – particularly given by anyone that promises you secrecy from the world's tax authorities. This is a double-edged sword – while the tax man may not know where your money is, you may not know either which makes the whole concern pretty pointless. A good simple test of a fund is to see whether any other similar fund, with a good reputation, has been registered in the same jurisdiction.

4. Is the fund audited by an accountancy practice of which you have heard?　　　　　　　　　Yes ☐ No ☐
Has it had an annual audit?　　　　　　　　　Yes ☐ No ☐

This is, of course, largely common sense – if an independent professional firm hasn't audited then you have no way of knowing whether anything the hedge

131

fund manager says is true. If the manager deals largely in the futures markets or in foreign exchange, you may get offered brokers' statements rather than an audit. This will give you an accurate picture of trading but any reputable firm will have an audit done as well.

5. Do you understand the prospectus or offering document? Yes ☐ No ☐

Again, this is largely common sense, but often one can get blinded by science and miss the obvious. Is the prospectus or offering document clear about what the hedge fund manager will do with your money, and does his past trading experiences bear out that this happened? Are you clear about the risks involved in the manager's trading? In particular, are you familiar with his approach to derivatives use, leverage or short sales? Do you know what market movements would make your manager vulnerable to losing money? What about fees? Do you understand what fees you will be charged and how much of the fund's overheads will come out of the investors' pockets?

6. Has the money under management in the fund grown significantly in recent months? Yes ☐ No ☐

Many asset managers find that while they can trade very successfully with a manageable size of money, if their assets get too big, they cannot find the trading opportunities and their performance is adversely affected. Ask if this is likely to be a problem if the manager you are considering has had a sharp increase in assets under management. Many of the sizable firms split their investment programs into various different styles, to keep funds at a manageable size, or simply close their funds to new investors. It may simply be an infrastructure concern – the firm may not have enough back office resources to cope with a large subscription. Ask how your investment will impact on the fund.

7. Has the actual manager of the money been with the firm for the past five years? Yes ☐ No ☐

Consistency in staff at a high level is considered essential by most investment professionals in the hedge fund field. Many of the investment strategies conducted by hedge fund managers require a personal, almost intuitive feel, developed by a manager over many years of trading. If investment success was merely based on making the right quantitative decisions then hedge fund managers would allow computers to trade for them while they were out on the golf course. Ensure that the fund and fund manager that attracted you in the first place is the one that you are going to get when you invest.

8. Are your phone calls and any other contact with the firm met with efficiency and politeness?   Yes ☐   No ☐

FRM indicates that in its experience there is a direct correlation between the quality of a fund's administrative infrastructure and the quality of the fund's returns. Something as simple as the efficiency or otherwise of the administrative staff can reveal a lot about the quality of the organization with which you are entrusting your money.

9. Will the hedge fund manager himself talk to you?   Yes ☐   No ☐

For the type of money that hedge fund managers command in minimum investments, the least they can do is talk to you. If you have any problems communicating with the person investing your money then you would have every right to be concerned. Investment managers usually provide references and it is important to follow these up as well. You could also talk to other investors or even the manager's competitors, who may give you the clearest picture of all.

10. Is the hedge fund manager's prospectus very expensively designed and printed?   Yes ☐   No ☐

This is the least serious of my points, but in my experience one can deduce a certain level of frivolity from a fund manager's literature. Lots of quotes from the wise and good of the past, lots of gold calligraphy, glassine sheets, handmade paper and exquisite artwork are all being paid for by the fund manager's business – which impacts on the investors' money. Similarly, I tend to distrust fund manager's offices that are incredibly plush – private, brass-appointed lifts, very deep-piled carpets and extensive wood panelling are a big worry. A hedge fund manager should be impressing you with his money management skills, not his interior decorating taste.

Scoring

Below 5 – think again.
5 to 8 – do more research.
8 and up – worthy of consideration.

Finally, here are some key issues to focus on when negotiating the investment management agreement between an investor and a hedge fund manager.

- To limit conflicts of interest, you should demand that all the managers' revenues are included in the fund's income and that the manager's involvement in other businesses is limited.
- You should seek to minimize lock-up periods to three months or less depending upon the investment strategy: it may be worth your while to agree to redemption fees on unscheduled redemptions.
- Since many strategies are limited in terms of the capital they can profitably employ, you should place a limit on the assets in the strategy.
- Regarding incentive fees, you should try to negotiate a hurdle rate as well as a cap on the absolute fees that can be paid to the manager. Because high water marks can work against investors, you should also try to negotiate multi-year rolling incentive fee schedules that will smooth out the manager's fees.
- Similarly, you should try to negotiate a cap on management fees. In the old days the main reason why hedge funds were able to get away with their high fee structure was because they were going to limit their asset size. One commentator says: "It is difficult to rationalize a 1% and 20% fee structure for funds managing large amounts of money. You should ask yourself whether the operating and other expenses of a fund managing $1bn exceed $10mn and whether the fund manager is able to invest that amount of money in targeted investments. Once an equity hedge manager is managing $1bn, he is beginning to look like a mutual fund manager." Management fees should not make the fund manager wealthy. At the very least, management fees should be subtracted from the incentive fee.

> **"Investors aren't just concerned with the probity of fund managers – their performance in terms of the investor's risk/reward profile is important too."**

Of course, investors aren't just concerned with the probity of fund managers – their performance in terms of the investor's risk/reward profile is important too. Thomas Schneeweis, professor of finance at the University of Massachusetts' Center for International Security and

Derivative Markets in the School of Management, researches the alternative investment fields. In his paper entitled, "Stock Funds, Bond Funds, Hedge Funds and Managed Futures Investments – How do they really differ?," Schneeweis stated the following:

... three simple rules of investment should be reviewed. First, an investment's expected return is related to its expected risk which may vary over different market environments. In short, not all stocks are riskier than all bonds, not all bonds are less risky than some managed futures or hedge fund investments, not all managed futures and hedge fund investments are riskier than all stock and bond investments. In simple terms, investor risk is the probability (i.e., chance) that an asset's value may change dramatically over some informationally variable investment period, and therefore, an asset's expected return should also vary over differing risk (e.g., informationally variable) environments.

Second, for the individual, investment risk is best measured as unexpected value changes due to unexpected changes in those factors (e.g., market environments) that affect an asset's value. For stocks, for instance, the increased chance of changes in firms' expected earnings per share or discount rate (i.e., risk-free interest rate plus risk premia) is an increase in investor risk. For instance, it is well known that on some days (i.e., days of economic release of money supply data for which there is uncertainty as to the value), that some stocks (i.e., bank stocks) and even some bonds are riskier (greater probability of price change) than other stocks (even high technology stocks unless those high technology stocks are funded by short term interest sensitive debt). What is the purpose of this example? Again, simply put, in the long run all assets offer expected returns that are commensurate with expected risk. However, since the risk of any investment is dependent on the conditions that are expected to exist over a particular investment period, likewise the expected returns of an investment are likewise dependent on unique informational and market conditions (e.g., liquidity) that are expected to exist over an investment period. As a result, different asset holdings will offer different expected returns in different market environments. While in the long run, one may expect stocks to earn a positive return commensurate with long run growth in a firm's earnings (or a portfolio of US stocks with GNP growth), over shorter investment periods, as expectations of future earnings growth or expected discount rate change, actual return may differ from those expected before the information change. Thus, in order to protect oneself from the inherent risk of alternative informational markets in which various kinds of stocks, bonds and other assets offer differing expected returns and risk, one may necessarily hold a wide range of alternative assets or investment strategies capable of capturing those changing risks (e.g., return opportunities).

Schneeweis goes on to say:

Basically, managed futures and hedge funds provide direct exposure to international investments and non-financial sectors such as commodities while offering through commodity trading advisors (through their ability to easily take both long and short investment positions) or hedge funds, whose investment style often requires investors to accept longer investment holding periods and thus enables them to hold less liquid asset positions, a means to gain exposure to risk and returns patterns not easily accessible with investment in traditional stock and bond portfolios.

THE HEDGE FUND
MANAGERS

Let the managers speak for themselves – here are interviews with four top hedge fund managers, responsible for investing billions of dollars. These profiles offer you a unique insight into the world of hedge funds and the investment minds behind them.

In this chapter, I interview four top hedge fund managers responsible for the investment management of billions of dollars. These profiles will give you an insight into how much of what I have already written about in this book works in practice and what type of fund managers become hedge fund managers.

Lee Ainslie of Maverick and Stephen Pearson of Sloane Robinson provided me with written answers to the questions and the others were interviewed. They all checked and had final approval on the copy.

MARKO DIMITRIJEVIC

Everest Capital

The first manager is Marko Dimitrijevic of Everest Capital Ltd. Everest Capital is a global value and special situations hedge fund with $2bn under management. Marko Dimitrijevic is the founder and president of the firm. He is 38, married with two children and was born and raised in Switzerland.

Despite its size, Everest is a very actively managed fund. Dimitrijevic uses his lengthy experience in investing to seek out investment opportunities. He takes great pleasure in finding "win/win" situations – investment strategies where both the long and the short offer good returns.

Please give your definition of a hedge fund.

I would define a hedge fund as a private fund, offered to a limited number of sophisticated individuals or institutional investors and I would add four sub-classifications:

1. It is a fund that seeks absolute, rather than relative returns.
2. It is a fund that has a lot of flexibility in being able to go long and short and use other hedging mechanisms
3. In a hedge fund, the manager makes the bulk of his compensation through an incentive fee structure, so the more the clients make the more the manager makes.
4. In a hedge fund, the manager has a high percentage of his own net worth invested in the fund alongside the investors, so that he shares on the downside if he makes bad decisions. This is essential, because otherwise if you have a manager that only has the incentive fee to earn from but nothing at risk – that's an invitation to gamble.

Please describe a little of the background to your business: how you started trading; what do you invest in; what is your current role?

I have always been in investment management since 1981 when I started working for a private Swiss bank doing international investment management. In 1983, I came to the US to do an MBA at Stanford University in California and then I began working on Wall Street for Paine Webber. I worked in high yield (junk bonds) research and mergers and acquisitions and learned a lot about analyzing special situations and company restructurings. I went on to manage money for Triangle Industries, investing in equities and high yield bonds and started Everest Capital in 1990. I set up Everest because I was always in the investment management business and saw an opportunity in doing a global hedge fund, applying things I learned in international investment management and on Wall Street, like how to look at companies from the standpoint of the buyer and using fundamental analysis plus hedging tools to decrease risk. I most enjoy investing.

> "I set up Everest because I was always in the investment management business and saw an opportunity in doing a global hedge fund."

My first two investors were my two previous bosses at Triangle and so that was a tremendous vote of confidence for me, and my boss at the Swiss bank also became an investor. We invest in four things:

1. Capital structure arbitrage where we take advantage of a discrepancy in the way the market values two securities of the same company or the same country. This is very attractive and very low risk because we have a good hedge in investing in the long and short from the same issuer. An example would be in the case of a company like Eurotunnel, where we were long the debt and short the stock. When the company stopped paying interest on the debt the stock went down so we profited from the short. Another example is Eurodisney where the company restructured on its debt with a rights offering which was diluted, which made the stock go down. But because the company was going to receive fresh cash the debt went up and the stock went down so we made money on both sides.

2. Value investing with a hedge – looking for cheap stocks or bonds and trying to find a catalyst that will bring the value out.

3. Value investing on the debt side – this is just like how we buy equities in value investing. We look for opportunities in distressed debt in the developed and emerging markets. Often there are better risk/reward ratios here than on equities.

4. Special situations, such as spin-offs, liquidations and various arbitrages.

We trade on a global basis, but the largest part is outside the US. Three years ago we launched a global emerging market hedge fund.

My current role with Everest is still managing the money, looking for opportunities to invest. We research through a variety of sources. We have a team of investment professionals who look for opportunities through research from major brokers in London and New York, plus local coverage and local brokers. We screen on our own for things that are cheap and attractive and a lot comes from monitoring the newspapers. The big opportunities are often there in the newspapers. Eurotunnel was on the front page of the *Financial Times* – anyone could read about it.

Do you have an image of a typical investor in your mind when you trade and if so, can you describe him or her?

My ideal investor is a long term investor who comes in and understands our strategies and is committed to staying with us for three to five years. We have sophisticated private investors and more and more long term institutions such as pension funds and endowments are coming in because they are looking for good returns with fairly low volatility. They also want low correlation to traditional investment management because the bulk of their funds is invested in traditional strategies. Our funds have produced superior returns with low correlations with the S & P or other major indices.

Is a hedge fund a superior investment vehicle for high net worth private investors and if so why?

Yes, because they seek absolute returns at the end of the day and people have forgotten how important that is after 15 years of bull markets in financial assets. But when we go back to a period of single digit or negative returns – then people will focus on hedge funds.

Also some of the most talented investment managers in the global fund industry go to the hedge fund format because of its flexibility. You have a free range of expression and if you

"A lot of talented people are in this sector."

are successful it is very lucrative – a lot of talented people are in this sector.

What can you offer that other hedge fund managers, of all types, can't?

I have been in the business for over 15 years and we have a lot of international experience. A lot of hedge funds are US based and our team is international and focused outside of the US. We think that there are better investment opportunities outside of the US because the research isn't as good. A lot of hedge funds focus only on equity markets and we've done a lot of things beside equities: particularly in the debt markets, whether corporate or sovereign, which broadens our opportunities and that is fairly unique.

How important is leverage to the performance of your hedge fund trading and what would your performance be like without it?

We don't use much leverage. We use the capability of shorting for hedging which creates leverage because you have more positions with the longs and the shorts combined – but it does cut the risk.

How do you personally assess risk in your trading?

Any time we take a position we look at how much we could lose on it and manage the size of the position based on that. The riskier it is, the smaller the position. In the portfolio, we also look at whether or how we can hedge a position. In capital structure arbitrage we look to see if we can short another security of the same company against a long, or in stock positions we may use an index or put options to limit the downside. Then we look at the risk after hedging a position and we look at the country risk and at the overall risk of the portfolio.

What are your best and worst experiences of trading?

The worst was in 1994 when many, many hedge funds lost money on leveraged bond trades and we did not. But other funds had large losses and experienced redemptions and had to sell some non-related securities and we held some of those securities which other hedge funds were selling. We didn't sell anything but the massive year-end selling made our positions go down so we had a loss in 1994 of down 5% over the year. It was frustrating because we were not down for fundamental reasons in our securities and we recovered in 1995.

My best experience of trading was to identify that there were tremendous opportunities in the Brady market after the Mexican devaluation at the end of 1994 and when the market crashed to a low in March 1995. Brady Bonds are restructured defaulted bank debt from the Latin American countries and some Eastern European sovereign debt. Brady Bonds are collateralized with US treasuries, reducing their risk. I was convinced that they were low risk opportunities. The market traded at incredibly cheap levels and then had a huge rally in 1995 and 1996.

What further goals in trading do you have?

I plan to continue with the same investment philosophy that has worked well over the past nine years. We are continuing to apply it. We'll never do anything for smaller investors because we don't need to: one fund is closed and we have to turn people down as it is. We are not interested in growing for the sake of growing and we have the majority of our own net worth invested in the fund, so it's very important that the fund continues to perform well.

JON M KNIGHT

Atlantic Portfolio Analytics & Management

The next profile is of Jon M Knight, chief investment officer of Atlantic Portfolio Analytics & Management Inc (APAM). APAM is a money manager that operates several hedge funds that primarily capture returns from a cash flow arbitrage between fixed income instruments, including mortgage backed securities and their derivatives, interest rate derivatives and US treasuries.

The mortgage backed securities market is one that few outside investors understand. Partly, this is because it is prone to acronyms and jargon, and partly because the mathematics involved in making investment decisions is quite specialized.

Knight says: "Investment decisions are based upon the optimization analysis of large scale simulations that integrate current information on market prices and volatilities with the cash flow and horizon pricing properties of a large list of candidate instruments. APAM rigorously incorporates the experience and market understanding of its staff into its models so that market knowledge is fully and consistently applied in the investment process."

Please give your definition of a hedge fund.

The traditional concept of a hedge fund has evolved. Originally, it was a vehicle that could hold both long and short positions to modify the volatility and correlation of its performance relative to that of the underlying markets. The current hedge fund contemplates combining the expanding list of balance sheet hedging instruments (swaps, caps, floors and options) with underlying securities and currencies to make levered bets on directional moves in markets or spreads. APAM prefers to characterize itself as a "hedged fund" rather than a hedge fund. We operate a number of funds and accounts that are levered and hedged to produce returns that are high and uncorrelated to the performance of underlying market indices over a defined holding period. This concept allows us to trade interim net asset value volatility for reliable long term above market returns.

Please describe a little of the background to your business: how you started trading; what do you invest in; what is your current role?

APAM was founded as a subsidiary of a bank in 1984 by Dr J Anthony Huggins, who had been Chief Economist and Investment Strategist for Florida's State Board of Administration, the agency which oversees the State's public employee pension fund. APAM managed the securities and liquidity of the bank and its insurance company subsidiaries. I joined APAM in 1986 as Director of Quantitative Analysis to develop CMO and cash flow arbitrage models for the asset/liability management strategy employed by the bank. I began trading in the mortgage derivatives market in 1987 while APAM was still a part of the bank. Dr Huggins and I bought the firm in 1988 and I became the Chief Investment Officer. We continued to manage the bank's portfolios and acquired asset management responsibilities for several other institutions. Toward the end of 1989 we embarked upon a concentrated research program in modern computational finance which paved our way into the hedge fund arena in 1991. Our initial funds basically levered an asset/liability matching strategy (originally developed for insurance companies) for offshore investors. We gained a number of clients that included separate accounts for institutions and ultra high net worth individuals. To avoid a proliferation of accounts that might become operationally inefficient, we consolidated our efforts in the limited number of hedge fund vehicles that we now manage.

I remain as Chief Investment Officer for APAM. As such I direct all investment activities which are carried out by two teams composed of about 20 professionals. The first team is the structuring team, which employs our analytical systems to (1) design portfolios and trades that offer well defined horizon return profiles and (2) quantify all components of risk to which our investors are exposed. The structuring team originates most of the trade ideas that are evaluated and approved by our investment management committee. The second team is the trading team. The traders are product specialist (IO/POs, floater/inverse floaters, passthroughs, fixed-coupon CMO/ABSs, treasuries, liquidity instruments, and interest rate derivatives) who not only execute all trades but who also provide daily assessments of market pricing and liquidity conditions. All trades are based upon a trading memorandum analyzed by the structuring team, endorsed by the investment management committee and approved by me.

Do you have an image of a typical investor in your mind when you trade and if so, can you describe him or her?

> **"A hedge fund is a superior investment vehicle."**

APAM managed hedge funds have an investor base that is diversified by type and geography. Investors include high net worth individuals and families, insurance companies and corporate pension funds from every region of the world. Our image of our investor base is directly reflected in our optimization models which fully characterize their return objectives and tolerance for all dimensions of risk.

Is a hedge fund a superior investment vehicle for high net worth private investors and if so why?

A hedge fund is a superior investment vehicle because it can provide exposure to a risk–return combination not available in long positions in any particular market. Thus the investor can exploit not only the added returns expected due to the skills of the manager chosen, but can also substantially diversify the overall performance risk with investments uncorrelated with the performance of the major asset classes.

What can you offer that other hedge fund managers, of all types, can't?

In formulating our strategies, we make a fundamental trade-off between:

1. The latent returns in excess of the costs of funding and hedging that can be extracted from a target sector of the fixed income market.
2. The degree of uncertainty in our ability to price securities at a horizon given the term structures of rates and volatilities.

3. How long we have to hold a position for the cheapness embedded in asset cash flow to dominate the uncertainty in projecting the returns to be captured.

This trade-off establishes a realistic horizon for constructing a reliable return profile versus the probable market exposure to which a portfolio will be subjected. We focus on developing the minimum cost hedge for a core portfolio to the defined horizon, accepting interim NAV volatility as the price of higher horizon returns. Our approach differs from most other hedge fund managers because APAM attempts to capture returns over a longer time horizon through collecting cheap cash flows rather than relying on nimble trading, directional biases, or price convergence to generate returns.

How important is leverage to the performance of your hedge fund trading and what would your performance be like without it?

I know of two ways to deliver high returns: one is leverage and the other is successful market timing. We have chosen to lever because we do not know how to predict reliably the short term direction of market prices. APAM generally leverages spreads and volatility in the mortgage, asset backed and interest rate derivatives markets employing various methods of financing. When we believe we can be over-compensated for bearing a component of risk, we will lever our exposure by buying intrinsically levered instruments (such as interest only strips and inverse floaters in the mortgage world) and by employing total return swaps, securities lending programs, and forward market transactions such as reverse repurchase agreements and so-called "dollar rolls."

How do you personally assess risk in your trading?

Since our portfolios are generally hedged against yield curve shifts, there are three primary sources of instantaneous changes in NAV:

- uncorrelated widening of spread products to their hedging basis;
- mismatches in key rate exposure along the curve; and
- larger changes in the term structure of (implied) volatility.

APAM generally structures levered portfolios to accept interim NAV volatility in trade for long term performance. We must, however, escape the revenge of the margin clerks under any circumstances, and we want to be able to treat market dislocation as a buying opportunity rather than a crisis. The key variable to manage, then, is available free collateral when the portfolio is under stress. Our regular risk management routine involves subjecting each portfolio to a set of stress test simulations that determine, after the stress test, how much liquidity would be available in the portfolio after we have met all margin calls attendant to the test. If free collateral in a portfolio is projected to drop below a predetermined level in a stress test simulation, it will be restructured to meet the liquidity standard.

What are your best and worst experiences of trading?

The worst of times were the best of times. The bond market massacre of 1994 and the associated collapse of Askin Capital Management left an indelible impression on everyone involved in the mortgage market. It was a period of extreme volatility which imposed the maximum stress placed on our people and systems to date. The market volatility was compounded first by a panicked and then by an aggressive assault by the dealer community on the ability of levered mortgage funds to hold and finance derivative positions. The net result was ultimately, of course, a general over-reaction in the market which brought quality assets into the market at very low prices. This opportunity allowed us to deliver extraordinary performance to our clients in the ensuing years.

What further goals in trading do you have?

APAM is aggressively pushing forward the state-of-the-art of our computational technology to model better and explore all of the niches of the markets in which we are engaged. Beyond this, we are pushing forward new approaches to sourcing cheap, high quality cash flows that can be hedged and financed.

Any other thoughts you wish to add?

While our approach is probably uncharacteristic of hedge fund operations, I think the most important benefit of the hedge fund market is to provide genuine diversification opportunities for investors.

LEE S AINSLIE III

Maverick Capital

The next interview is with Lee S Ainslie III who is the managing partner of Maverick Capital. Maverick Capital is a traditional long/short equity hedge fund with $1.5bn under management. Thirty-three year old Lee Ainslie is the managing partner. He is married with one child. Ainslie has been described as "running the best conservative Jones model fund we know of, barring none!" by *Lookout Mountain Hedge Fund Review*.

Please give your definition of a hedge fund.

The term "hedge fund" has come to represent a wide variety of investment vehicles; many of which make little or no attempt to be hedged. Indeed, the strategy and performance of many of these funds is driven by non-hedged investments. Of course, there are many ways to add value and make money, and nothing is wrong with unhedged investing. I just disagree with the nomenclature.

I tend to use the term "hedge fund" in a more old-fashioned sense – funds that actively hedge, or reduce, market and other macroeconomic risks. As a result, the performance of such funds is driven by their ability to select individual securities, not by market timing or by the performance of different markets or market sectors. In analyzing different investment vehicles, investors should understand how different funds and strategies add value and create performance and draw their own conclusions as to the sustainability of the returns of different strategies.

Please describe a little of the background to your business: how you started trading; what do you invest in; what is your current role?

Maverick Capital was started in 1990 by the Wyly family to manage their personal assets. By 1993, they had achieved annualized returns in excess of 40% and decided to turn their investment activity into a business and accept outside investors. Before doing so, they wanted to bring in more professional money management experience and they contacted me.

I have been looking at stocks since joining an investment club in seventh grade. My big break came when Julian Robertson of Tiger hired me out of business school. Of course, I am eternally grateful to Julian for the opportunity and education he gave me. Like most people who follow Tiger, my tremendous respect for his abilities and achievements continues to grow year by year. I left Tiger to join the Wylys in August of 1993, and we started to accept outside investors that October. In February of 1995, I took over as the sole fund manager of the two Maverick funds.

Today, I continue to be responsible for all final investment decisions, but I am surrounded by a group of very talented and experienced peers – Lee Hobson, Michael Au, Steve Kapp, Mike Pausic and Duke Buchan – who are instrumental in most investment decisions. From a business standpoint, Maverick is controlled by two managing partners, Evan Wylys and myself. As the Wyly family continues to be the largest investor in Maverick, Evan's role ensures that our investors' interests are paramount in every decision. I was very fortunate to team up with the Wylys – Maverick would clearly not be as successful today without their guidance and support over the years.

> **"We have simply shifted most of our macroeconomic risk to security selection risk."**

Maverick's solitary goal is to preserve and grow capital. We believe that over the long-term the best way to achieve this goal will be to manage the fund in a truly hedge fashion. We have taken this hedged strategy a step further than many in that we maintain consistent, low net exposure to each region and industry sector in which we invest. By doing so, Maverick's performance is driven by our ability to select securities, rather than trying to time markets or pick hot regions or industries. Importantly, Maverick only invests in long and short equities and does not invest in bonds, commodities, currencies, futures or other derivatives. This strategy is designed to focus our efforts where we add the most value – picking stocks.

By being hedged within each region and industry, Maverick has greatly reduced a variety of risks including market, currency, interest rate and other macroeconomic risks. This is not to say that this is a lower risk strategy. By being so diligently hedged, we have simply shifted most of our macroeconomic risk to security selection risk. We have purposefully shifted our risk profile as we believe that through intensive fundamental analysis, individual securities are inherently more predictable than markets. Furthermore, we recognize that the greatest talent and experience of the Maverick team lies in security selection, and we want all our efforts focused purely on picking stocks.

To be hedged, Maverick typically maintains net market exposure between 20% and 60% of net assets. In other words for every $100 invested in Maverick, typically only $20 to $60 is invested net long in the equity markets. Over the last four years, our average net exposure has been 43%. Our short exposure is created purely through shorting individual securities, rather than by shorting index futures or by buying index puts. Although this practice is increasingly unusual, shorting stocks rather than indices allows us to add value and improve performance by selecting securities that we believe will perform worse than the market. Frankly, most of our investors are sophisticated enough that they can buy puts and sell futures themselves, if they are just looking to lower exposure. By consistently maintaining net exposure in this low positive range, we have struck a balance between reducing the inherent disadvantages of the short side and keeping low enough exposure to have virtually no correlation to the market. Our r-squared, or degree of correlation to the market, of this hedged strategy has been just 9% – anything under 40% is typically considered uncorrelated.

As I mentioned, by maintaining low net exposure in every region and in every industry, we have greatly reduced macroeconomic risk but have greatly increased security selection risk. Recognizing this, we work hard to mitigate this stock-picking risk in several ways. The funds are quite diversified with typically over 150 investments. We use very strict position size limits – no long position is ever greater than 6% of net assets and no short is ever greater than 3%. Finally, we adhere very strictly to a series of loss limit rules, which are designed to help us recognize the difference between opportunities and mistakes. These practices, together with our hedged approach, have helped us to achieve significant returns with a great deal of consistency and relatively little volatility.

Now this long winded response tells you how we invest, but I did not really answer your question: "What do you invest in?" The quick answer is stocks. Of course, in selecting securities many different models and methodologies are useful, and in my judgement the ability to choose which analysis is appropriate for which situation is the most important element in picking stocks. So generalizing how we select securities can be a bit dangerous because I promise you that at any one time we will have several positions which do not fit every parameter I discuss.

Having said that, here are a few of the factors on which we concentrate. On the long side, we invest in strong fundamental businesses with solid competitive positions. We try to understand the key internal and external drivers to a business, and we evaluate our ability to monitor these drivers. The ability of a company to generate true free cash flow on a sustainable basis and the ability to reinvest this capital with significant returns is critical. Management's demonstrated commitment to maximize shareholder value is a driving factor in this evaluation of capital deployments.

> "Comparing sustainable free cash flow to the enterprise value of an entity is our most commonly used valuation paradigm."

Indeed, we are very focused on the quality of management and consider ourselves partners with the management teams in which we are invested. In the due diligence process, we spend an inordinate amount of time verifying that the leaders of these companies have the integrity, intelligence and desire to create shareholder value that we believe is critical to the success of a long term investment.

I strongly believe that every stock has an underlying economic value and that the market will realize this value over time. So our valuation efforts are focused on recognizing discrepancies between the market's current valuation and our estimate of true economic value. Comparing sustainable free cash flow to the enterprise value of an entity is our most commonly used valuation paradigm.

As you might expect, on the short side we are searching for the opposite – poor fundamental businesses in weak competitive positions hopefully with mediocre management. In today's extraordinarily competitive global markets, weak management teams are bound to stumble eventually. Valuation is a much less important consideration in evaluating potential shorts. In other words, we do not short companies simply because they are overvalued, as such valuation discrepancies may persist for years. Furthermore, we tend to avoid popular or crowded shorts as these situations can be dangerous in the short-term if a squeeze develops and less profitable in the long term as so much pent-up buying demand exists.

Over time, the consistent application of these fundamentals has led to very strong stock-picking results. Even on an unleveraged basis, our longs have outperformed the market every single year and our shorts have underperformed the market every single year. As we discussed, our performance is driven by this ability to pick longs that will do better than the market, and shorts that will do worse. So far, we have consistently done so and hope to continue such performance going forward.

Do you have an image of a typical investor in your mind when you trade and if so, can you describe him or her?

If by "investor" you are referring to an investor in Maverick, then there really is no typical investor. We, the partners of Maverick, and related entities are the biggest investors in the funds with roughly $200m invested. Other individuals make up almost 40% of our capital base and the remainder has been invested by a range of corporations, banks, insurance companies, educational endowments, pensions, foundations, etc., from almost very corner of the globe. All these assets are treated as one pool of capital, so all our efforts are focused on just one set of decisions that impact on all investors equally. We spend a great deal of time educating potential investors to ensure that we only accept individuals and entities who understand our approach and share our goal of preserving and growing capital, creating one common denominator in our investor base.

If by investor you are referring to other investors in the equity markets, then again I am not sure if there is any such thing as a typical investor. I tend to think of the market as the world's most efficient polling mechanism which is dollar weighted. In other words, all investors have the opportunity to "vote" with dollars creating the supply/demand balance that determines the price of a security. We recognize that in the short term the supply and demand for a security can be driven by a multitude of factors, many of which may be of little long term consequence or which may be the result of emotional rather than logical decisions. Furthermore, I believe that investors tend to either under-react or over-react, but rarely react appropriately to new developments or surprises. This is why contrarian investing can prove to be so rewarding. By developing a thorough understanding of the fundamentals of a company and strong relationships with management teams, we hope to be able to understand the true long-term impact of different events. By doing so, we attempt to take advantage of both panic and overly exuberant situations or short term mispricings. To be able to react this way, and disagree with the rest of the world, requires confidence in our long term analysis and judgement.

> **"Do you understand how the fund invests and makes money?"**

Is a hedge fund a superior investment vehicle for high net worth private investors and if so why?

Since the vast bulk of my net worth is invested in a single hedge fund (I will let you guess which one), I would have to answer "yes." However, like most things in life, hedge funds do not bear generalizations very well. As the number of hedge funds continues to skyrocket every day, the quality of funds has become more mixed. Some funds have developed a strategy and a track record deserving of a large portion of an individual's net worth, and others probably deserve none. So, I think that question must be analyzed on a fund by fund basis.

In determining if an investment in a particular fund is appropriate, I would focus on several questions. Does the fund deliver either superior performance with equivalent risk to the market, or equivalent performance with lower risk? About the only common denominator I find in hedge funds is that they all charge some type of performance fee – is this fee justified? How does the fund generate performance, and how sustainable is this process? And in order to assess the prior question accurately – do you understand how the fund invests and makes money?

THE HEDGE FUND MANAGERS

Theoretically, a hedge fund should be able to meet these criteria and have the capability to be a "superior investment vehicle." Hedge funds have much more flexibility than most investment vehicles, and most employ strategies that should allow them to generate superior performance, a better risk profile or both. Furthermore, a performance fee ensures that the manager is incentivized and motivated to perform, whereas a straight management fee rewards asset growth rather than performance. Not only does the fee structure properly align the manager's motivations to those of his investor, but also the economics of a hedge fund vehicle have attracted many of the hardest working and most talented money managers.

What can you offer that other hedge fund managers, of all types, can't?

At Maverick, we do not possess any secret formula or magical black box that guarantees our ability to add value. Our success has been the result of hard work and intensive analysis by a very talented and experienced team which has applied an intelligent, straightforward strategy in a very disciplined manner. The prototype for our strategy, which I described earlier, was started by A W Jones in the late 1940s – we have simply refined Mr Jones' original hedged approach to include stronger risk control and to bring greater focus to our efforts on security selection. In terms of analyzing long and short investments, again we do not possess a unique crystal ball. The Maverick team constantly scours the earth for the companies with the best and worst business fundamentals, competitive positions, management teams and valuations. Like many investors, we pore over financial statements, use a variety of valuations methodologies, develop relationships with management teams, and speak with the customers, suppliers and competitors of potential investments.

However, we do believe that the Maverick strategy, our disciplined focus, the Maverick team and the success we have achieved in both preserving and growing capital are all unique characteristics of Maverick Capital. We are not aware of any imitators of our approach, and I believe this stems from the fact that this strategy requires superior stock-picking to generate returns. Our performance is driven by our ability to select longs which will outperform the market and shorts which will underperform – this requires much more effort and talent than simply riding the upward trend that the market has enjoyed over the last several years, but which may not continue.

As we discussed, we are focused where we add the most value. Many funds now employ a multitude of strategies and invest in a variety of securities. Frankly, I believe that we have the ability to successfully invest in other strategies and other securities, but I believe that we would prove to be much better at investing in equities, so we choose to focus all our energies on this skill. Our strategy requires a great deal of discipline, but we do not stray from this strategy nor shy away from that discipline.

The Maverick team is the most important factor in our success. We have been fortunate to attract a very bright, talented and experienced team of peers with a strong blend of industry and investment experience. One of the many important lessons Julian Robertson taught me is that a reputation for the utmost integrity is a critical asset in the investment business. Although such qualities are difficult to determine from looking at performance numbers or reading resumés, the ethical character of each member of the Maverick team is a vital factor in our success. The diligent efforts of this team and the strategy with which we invest have achieved results with a risk/return profile that we believe is rather unique.

How important is leverage to the performance of your hedge fund trading and what would your performance be like without it?

That depends on how one defines "leverage". If the term "leverage" represents borrows then Maverick uses relatively little. Typically, Maverick only borrows approximately 25% of our equity so borrows are not an important factor in our performance Indeed the cash balances resulting from our short sales are typically more than three times the size of our borrows.

Many think of the term "leverage" as "total capital at risk", whether invested with or against the market, in comparison to equity – I refer to this as "gross exposure." At Maverick, gross exposure is roughly two to one, or 200% and is an integral component of our strategy. If for every $200 invested, the fund invests $120 in long securities and $80 in short securities, then Maverick would have net exposure of $40 ($120 – $80) or 40% and gross exposure of $200 ($120 + $80) or 200%. Having gross exposure of 200% or more allows us to maintain that short exposure, which of course is fundamental to our hedged strategy. Indeed, one of the significant advantages of a truly hedged strategy is the ability to leverage the invested capital while decreasing the market risk. So what would our performance be like with lower gross exposure? The answer to that question could vary greatly depending on how such a reduction was implemented.

How do you personally assess risk in your trading?

In a number of different ways. First, as we discussed, Maverick monitors and reduces macroeconomic risk by maintaining low net exposure within every region and every industry in which we invest. These ratios are measured daily and are calculated on a *pro forma* basis every day for the following day's trading plan of action. These net exposure levels are also measured on a beta-adjusted basis.

Security selection risk is assessed and mitigated in several ways. Our systems monitor position size limits, a series of strict loss limit rules and diversification requirements. Importantly, we pay a great deal of attention to our mistakes; so our risk control methodologies are very focused on securities, regions or industry sectors which are not performing as expected. Finally, our systems monitor the short term impact of every trading decision, allowing us to see the impact of every investment we have made during the month. This has proven to be a great tool in improving our trading abilities

What are your best and worst experiences of trading?

I can think of so many bad experiences that it is hard to chose. However, almost every bad experience I recall proved to be an educational experience. In the investment business, one makes so many decisions every day that there will be an abundance of mistakes. To be a successful investor, I believe that the ability to recognize mistakes and then to learn from those mistakes is absolutely essential.

If I had to pick just one regrettable experience, I would dredge up a bad memory from years ago – the large ownership of a software company whose stock price was cut in half in a single day after pre-announcing disappointing earnings. In an environment where every senior member participates in the success of the firm and the firm's fees are based on performance, such a loss is devastating because you have taken money out of the pockets of both your investors and your peers.

In this case, l had developed a nice relationship and great respect for the management team and was too willing to listen to their confident reassurances. This confidence was confirmed by relationships I had developed with board members and regional salesmen of the company. I was therefore shocked to learn that earnings would be less than half of Wall Street's and my expectations. Of course, the entire investment community had a similar reaction, and the stock was decimated.

The "autopsy" revealed that I had not been intentionally misled, rather the company's internal forecasting system was not able to keep pace with the changing nature of their business. My sales contacts were correct about the strength of their own business, but much of the revenue shortfall came in the company's European operations were I did not have such relationships. Given the operating leverage in the business, the dramatically weak earnings were actually the result of a rather small, roughly 10%, revenue miss.

> "One can never have too many sources and relationships to continually check and double-check the key drivers of a business."

A couple of important lessons were reinforced by this experience. Developing a strong relationship with a capable and ethical management team does not always mean that you are receiving good information. Secondly, one can never have too many sources and relationships to continually check and double-check the key drivers of a business. I did realize, however, that the dramatic price decline was not commensurate with the decline in the business. Indeed this price drop proved to be unjustified as the company was sold within a year for a per-share price almost triple that of the nadir. This sale reinforced a final lesson – the importance of investing with a board and a management team committed to realizing shareholder value.

Although I have been fortunate to have a few successful stocks over the years, my best experience in trading, both in terms of enjoyment and performance, has been Maverick's ownership of a retail stock over the last three years. I had been short this stock off and on over the years, primarily because I felt that the company had made several strategic blunders and was being run in a non-economic fashion. As the company headed towards bankruptcy, the board recognized that a management shake-up was necessary. They bought in a new CEO whom we knew and respected from his prior position.

I always felt that this retailer had significant growth potential given that it was the dominant retailer and brand name in one of the fastest-growing consumer products – computers. I also felt that the rise of the Internet, the lower price points of computers and the increasing ease of use of software would drive huge consumer demand. So when after several months on the job the new CEO made difficult, but in our judgement, critical management changes, our interest was piqued.

We ended up taking a small position at 1 7/8 on today's basis, but continued to increase that position over the next two years as we recognized the power of the long term vision and how effectively and rapidly this plan was being implemented. Management moved quickly to rationalize and streamline the basic business. Our conversations with the company's suppliers and competitors, as well as our visits to many stores around the country, confirmed that the company was making dramatic improvements and was back on the right track. After literally saving the company, the new management team began to expand both the sales and the profitability of the business by introducing new services and products that leveraged off the store base and brand name.

Today this retailer has reached a critical mass, a profitability model and a return on capital unmatched in their industry. As a result they have debilitated their competition and are positioned to extend their dominance throughout the US. In my judgement, this has been one of the most stunning turnarounds in retail history and we have been very fortunate to partake of their success. Even though the stock is up almost 20-fold since our initial purchase, it is still one of our favorite investments.

Just as we try to learn from our mistakes, we also study our successes in the hope of improving our odds of repeating such success. In this case, the marriage of a well-positioned, but neglected, asset and a driven shareholder oriented manager proved to be quite fruitful. Although turnarounds are riskier, they are more likely to be home runs when you are right. In this case, we were willing to increase our investment at substantially higher prices as we saw the fundamentals of the business continue to improve. I believe it is paramount to focus on where a stock is going, rather than where it has been. This stock certainly fulfilled the old adage that "the next double is easier than the last."

What further goals in trading do you have?

The goal of Maverick Capital is to grow and preserve our capital. As we discussed, we believe that the best way to achieve this goal will be to continue to invest in equities in a truly hedged manner. Not only do I believe that this is where we add the most value, but picking stocks also happens to be what I enjoy the most.

Personally my goal is to continue to improve my abilities as an investor. One of the most enjoyable and challenging aspects of this profession is that one always has the opportunity to learn about different industries, trading strategies, management teams, valuation methodologies, etc. Longer-term, my goal is to continue to build an organization and a track record of which I can be proud.

Any other thoughts you wish to add?

As hedge funds continue to attract more and more capital from both high net worth and institutional investors, I hope that these investors have a thorough understanding of the strategies in which they have invested. Furthermore, as funds continue to proliferate I hope investors conduct sufficient due diligence on individual managers. Investors who have not done their homework or who do not fully comprehend the strategies to which they have committed their capital, run the risk of an unhappy surprise.

STEPHEN PEARSON

Sloane Robinson Investment Management

The next profile is of Sloane Robinson Investment Management and the interview was done with Stephen Pearson. He is one of the four hedge fund managers who look after investment in Japan, Asia, emerging markets and Europe. Sloane Robinson was established because its principals had found the traditional requirements of the institutional fund management industry very frustrating. Not interested in providing benchmarked returns, Sloane Robinson aims to use stock-picking skills to achieve absolute returns. Sloane Robinson is an international equity hedge fund with close to $3bn of assets under management.

Please give your definition of a hedge fund.

The prerequisite of a hedge fund is an absolute return focus rather than relative returns to a stated index benchmark. The implications or symptoms of this are that hedge funds have wider investment powers allowing them to use leverage, derivative instruments, short selling of individual stocks and so on. They also have a portfolio construction which is substantially different from the traditional benchmark weightings and a return profile which is substantially different from traditional indices.

The defining features of Sloane Robinson's style of trading are that we diversify by themes, industries and individual stocks – which means that we run effectively diversified portfolios holding 60–80 individual equities, encompassing eight to 12 separate non-correlated investment themes, both long and short. No individual holding represents more than 5% of NAV at cost. Our portfolios are therefore diversified from a risk of losing money perspective, not from a risk of underperforming the index perspective.

Our second defining feature, which is specific to us, is the restrictions that we place on our ability to use leverage. Our restrictions are 135% long in stocks, 100% in asset allocation overlay in stock index futures and 100% hedged back to dollars. All of these are maximums, not the norm, and this is particularly true with the stock index futures which are principally used to insure the portfolios rather than to gear them up. We use stock index futures principally to protect our portfolios against an adverse move rather than to amplify a positive move or an upward move.

Our third defining feature is that SR is run along a partnership structure. All the directors are invested in the fund; all the directors have a significant proportion of their net worth in the funds which ensures a strong fusion of interest with our clients. From a business point of view this means that our focus as a company is naturally on an asset management not an asset gathering footing.

> **"Trading plays a minimal part in our activities."**

Please describe a little of the background to your business: how you started trading; what do you invest in; what is your current role?

SR was established at the end of 1993 by George Robinson and Hugh Sloane. Robinson was the head of research at W I Carr in the Far East. Sloane was investment director at LGT Asset Management in Tokyo and London. Stephen Pearson joined in April 1994 (also from LGT), Richard Chenevix-Trench (formerly head of emerging markets investment at Barings) in January 1996 and Mark Haworth in January 1996 from LGT, where he was a European investment manager. All of the principals are from an investment, rather than a trading, background. Trading plays a minimal part in our activities. Roughly 75% of our time is spent analyzing companies, meeting with management, writing internal investment reports (we have developed our own in-house analytical database). We invest principally in equities in Europe, the Far East and Latin America, which means that in US parlance we are an international equity manager.

Our investment disciplines combine top-down economic and stock market analysis with bottom-up stock-picking. From the top-down we look at liquidity trends in an economy (we produce our own in-house economic research product monthly), earnings momentum and valuations (price/book, price/cash, etc., both in absolute terms and relative to the 10-year history). From the bottom-up we hold regular meetings with company management and stockmarket analysts at our offices and undertake local investment trips to review investment opportunities, meet with companies and political or central bank representatives.

In terms of responsibility at SR, Hugh Sloane is investment director with additional responsibility for stock selection in Japan, George Robinson is responsible for Asia, Richard Chenevix-Trench for emerging markets and Stephen Pearson (assisted by Mark Haworth) for Europe.

Do you have an image of a typical investor in your mind when you trade and if so, can you describe him or her?

Our typical investor is a high net worth private individual, a charitable foundation or a family office. Someone with a medium to long term investment horizon and a strong aversion to losing money. We have provided compounded annual returns of roughly between 20 and 30% a year since inception.

Is a hedge fund a superior investment vehicle for high net worth private investors and if so, why?

Our experience would say, "Yes it is," because our clients hate losing money more than they hate underperforming an index. But it also depends on the individual's risk/return investment objectives and the investment policy of the individual hedge fund. SR seeks to deliver 15–20% annual returns over the longer term with low annual downside risk. Some years, returns may be low (both in absolute and relative terms) but annual drawdowns should be small in bad times and occasionally, maybe once in five years, there should be the opportunity to utilize the fund's investment powers to make more substantial returns – say 35% plus.

What can you offer that other hedge fund managers, of all types, can't?

We have no secret proprietary systems or techniques to guarantee success. We have a clear investment philosophy and defined method for implementation and risk control. Risk adjusted performance and the integrity of our employees can be our only competitive advantages.

How important is leverage to the performance of your hedge fund trading, and what would your performance be like without it?

See above in answer to the first question for the degree of leverage that we use. It's not very important to our trading and we don't disaggregate performance in this way. Leverage is used to hedge the portfolios, not to speculate. A leveraged position, in the sense of the gross balance sheet position, is used to hedge, so is composed of both long and short positions.

How do you personally assess risk in your trading?

Short term trading plays a minimal part in our implementation of investment ideas. All our investments are considered from a perspective of the risk of losing money. Absolute stock price targets are held for all investments (long and short). Position sizes in individual stocks are used to regulate the risk.

What are your best and worst experiences of trading?

Our worst experiences of trading are October 1997 and September 1995 when periods of sharp and volatile stockmarket moves have caused us to insure the portfolio against further losses unnecessarily. Our best experiences came through the implementation of a top-down call on the Italian market in the first quarter of 1997 through stocks and index futures.

Our worst experiences in investment are when individual stocks go wrong. When this happens, it is most commonly a result of management disinformation. Our best experiences in investment are when the combination of identifying value in a sector or individual company is compounded by correctly identifying the macro conditions for that country. When the micro meets the macro is the most rewarding investment scenario for us. Good examples of that have been in Russia, in the electrical utilities, in Poland, in banks, and on the short side, in South-East Asia, in Thai financials, for example.

What further goals in trading do you have?

Our goals on trading are primarily capital preservation. From a business point of view, our goals are to deliver on our promises to clients rather than to grow our assets under management or to proliferate our products.

Any other thoughts you wish to add?

While the growth in the hedge fund niche in Europe is exciting, it's important that people who are providing the capital to support these funds understand the nature of the investments and the return profile that those investments are likely to generate. I think it's worrying that clients think that they can both outperform strongly rising markets and never lose money. Those are two inconsistent investment objectives.

PAUL MARSHALL

Marshall Wace Asset Management Ltd

The last interview was conducted over the telephone with Paul Marshall. Marshall Wace is a new European hedge fund manager established in 1998.

Please give your definition of a hedge fund.

There are many different types of hedge funds corresponding to the many segments within the hedge fund industry, but there are two defining characteristics which make hedge funds identifiable. First, their objective – hedge funds seek absolute rather than relative returns. Second, the means that they employ – hedge funds employ many more tools than traditional investment managers of which the most important tool is the ability to go short. Ultimately the defining characteristic of a hedge fund is its ability to go short.

Please describe a little of the background to your business: how you started trading; what do you invest in; what is your current role?

Ian Wace and I have known each other for 12 years. We both began our careers in the SG Warburg group, Ian working on the securities side and myself working in fund management. For most of the 1980s,

Ian and I knew each other as broker and client. Ian became the head of European sales at Warburgs and I became chief investment officer for European equities at Mercury Asset Management. In the 1990s, Ian moved to create and subsequently head European, then International, proprietary trading at SG Warburg with considerable success and then he went on to become head of global equity trading and risk at Deutsche Morgan Grenfell.

I had wanted to move into the hedge fund business for a number of years, but I believe that managing money for absolute returns is very different from managing money for relative returns. It requires a different mind set and a different risk management platform. I have seen traditional managers try to produce an absolute return product by cobbling together a group of relative return managers with some big asset allocation overlays and it doesn't work. So, this is why I have joined together with Ian who has been breathing and sleeping absolute returns for the last seven years. He knows how to manage risk, how to trade and how to short. We started talking in early 1997 and left our jobs in June 1997, launching the Eureka Fund in January 1998. We currently have $170m under management and we were up 18% at the end of May 1998.

Our fund seeks to generate skill-based returns by investing and trading in quoted European equities – basically Western European equities. We aim to generate these returns regardless of the market environment and would therefore expect the fund's returns to have a low correlation to market movements.

We use fundamental analysis for all positions and we target event-driven situations. We draw an intellectual distinction between investment positions and trading positions. The investment positions consist of exceptional businesses which generate super normal returns on invested capital and will usually have high growth characteristics. We would hope to hold these for long periods and we have a core of such positions which represent up to 50% of NAV.

Trading positions are more opportunistic and we have identified a number of catalysts which we believe will trigger good trading opportunities. The most important of these are mergers and acquisitions; technical situations (e.g., stock overhangs, rights issues), capital restructuring and deregulation (a good source of short ideas). The trading book will normally consits of much shorter term positions and is designed to generate a stream of consistent capital gains to smooth the performance of the fund.

Given our backgrounds – I have a bias towards the investment positions and Ian towards the trading strategies – we believe strongly in a four eyes principal and review all investment and trading strategies together before taking any action.

I spend much more time on the road than Ian, visiting companies, while Ian acts as the guardian of the profit and loss, particularly in relation to risk management. Our respective roles play to our strengths. My background is in investment analysis and research and I spend most of my time analysing companies, visiting companies all around Europe.

Do you have an image of a typical investor in your mind when you trade and if so, can you describe him or her?

Our typical, and also ideal, investor is a high net worth individual who wishes to participate in the opportunities available in the equity markets but with those returns not dependent upon the markets' performance. Our investors should expect a consistent and steady appreciation of their capital with the confidence of down-side protection from adverse market movements.

Is a hedge fund a superior investment vehicle for high net worth private investors and if so why?

A hedge fund is the superior investment vehicle for high net worth private investors and that is why the hedge fund industry has grown so explosively. To understand why, you first have to understand how high net worth clients' investments have been managed historically. There have essentially been two main alternatives for such investors. First, there has been the option of having their money managed on an advisory basis through a private equity broker in the churn and burn tradition. This approach produces a clear conflict of interest as the objective of the broker is to maximise commissions and many private investors have ended up dissatisfied with the total return.

The second approach is to have your money managed in the private client department of a large investment management firm. This avoids the commission problem. But in most cases the private client department will manage the money for relative returns, cloning the investment strategy of the institutional department of the same firm. So if the market is down 20% and the clients have lost 18%, the manager thinks he has done a good job. The hedge fund offers a fundamentally different product to both these approaches.

First, far from there being a conflict of interest between hedge fund manager and client, the hedge fund manager will have invested most if not all of his private wealth in the fund, thereby fully aligning his interests with that of his customers. In addition the vast majority of his remuneration is linked to the performance of the assets. No performance – no fee.

Second, the hedge fund will be unequivocally managed for absolute return, and in the case of most hedge funds (sadly not all) a strong emphasis on capital preservation. Third, hedge fund managers are entirely focused on the performance of their fund and not distracted by office politics and management committees. Finally, the hedge fund manager has more tools in his tool box than traditional managers. In addition to the normal buy and hold strategy, the hedge fund manager is able to short, to trade and to gear.

What can you offer that other hedge fund managers, of all types, can't?

There are over 5000 hedge funds in the US, many run by highly skilled investors. We would not want to claim to be able to offer something unique compared with that universe. However the European picture is different. There are only a small number of hedge funds and we believe that we offer a unique combination of skills – investment analysis, research, trading and risk management. We have developed our own risk management platform which we believe is at the cutting edge, certainly in Europe. We have developed an outstanding operational infrastructure and lastly we have made considerable efforts to ensure a high level of transparency for our clients.

(One of the frustrations for private clients investing in hedge funds can be the lack of transparency. We have sought to overcome this with a website with protected access for our clients so that they can see on a daily basis the performance, the market exposure and the core holdings of our fund.)

How important is leverage to the performance of your hedge fund's trading and what would your performance be like without it?

Gross gearing (i.e., the ability to go long and short and to use balance sheet leverage) is very important as it allows us to optimise skill based returns. Net gearing is not very important (i.e., going more than 100% long). Net gearing is allowed in the prospectus but we will rarely be over 100% invested and mostly between 50 and 70% net long.

How do you personally assess risk in your trading?

We measure risk on six dimensions:

- Individual portfolio exposures on a stock and country basis, i.e. no individual holding can represent more than 20% of net asset value.
- Net market exposure shall not exceed the limit of −50% to 130%.
- Gross gearing: we have set ourselves a limit of 400%.
- Portfolio liquidity shall not exceed three trading days. We are not prepared to sacrifice liquidity for performance. This means that if we wanted to liquidate the portfolio we could do it within three trading days.
- Beta-adjusted exposures. The net market exposure can often be misleading as it does not capture the characteristics of long and short positions. Beta-adjusted is not a perfect measure in itself but comes closer to catching the characteristics of the portfolio. We also beta-test the portfolio to track the actual beta over the holding period, enabling us to better hedge the risk.
- Value at risk – expected volatility of the portfolio based on 250 trading days shall not exceed 2.5 times. In practice it's not been above 1.2.

What are your best and worst experiences of trading?

It's a little early to answer this question. However, a good experience of trading so far has been our investment in Seat. Seat owns and publishes the Italian yellow pages. It also publishes the Italian telephone directory (white pages) on behalf of Telecom Italia and has a number of smaller activities in direct marketing and specialised publishing. With its quasi-monopoly position and exceptional franchise in Italy, we could classify Seat as an investment grade stock (ROIC 25%). But it was also a special situation with a number of catalysts to trigger performance.

Seat was spun off from Stet in January 1997. The Italian Treasury received 61.3% of the ordinary shares and subsequently (November 1997) sold its majority control to a leveraged consortium of venture capitalists and banks called Otto. This was another example of European politicians selling the family silver on the cheap. Otto paid an EV/EBITBA of six times. Two months later, VNU acquired the Benelux yellow pages for an EV/EBITBA of 11.1 times and the market applauded VNU.

Meanwhile, back in Italy, the market waited for Otto to issue its tender offer for the outstanding minorities of Seat at the knock-down price of LIT 710, and effectively forgot about the stock.

By February 1998, Otto had still not issued its tender offer, Italian interest rates had tumbled and VNU had shown the real value of a yellow pages franchise. The price of Seat had remained unchanged at the level of Otto's tender offer. What the market forgot was that the minorities were not required to accept the Otto tender offer. On our estimates the stock was worth close to double the share price of LIT 710 (the forthcoming tender offer price).

At the beginning of March we put 9% of the fund into Seat. The share price more or less doubled in the space of eight weeks.

Our worst experience is the generally sobering experience of shorting shares in bull markets!

What further goals in trading do you have?

We are constantly striving to improve our understanding of portfolio dynamics. Historic volatilities are not much better as a guide to future volatilities than historic returns are as a guide to future returns. Therefore any risk management system based on historic data will have limitations to its predictive power. We try to optimise our exposures and also the symmetry between longs and shorts on a daily basis so that the overall returns have as little correlation to market movements as possible. This is an ongoing enterprise.

Any other thoughts you wish to add?

Investors in Western markets have been spoilt by a bull market that has now gone on for almost an investment generation. It is remarkable that hedge funds have gained such support against such an investment background.

When we go into a period of two or three years when markets don't deliver, then people will look to skill based strategies even more and there will be an explosion in the growth of the hedge fund industry. In 10 years' time hedge funds will be an entirely established and accepted part of the investment management scene. The investment management industry will be increasingly polarized between the whales and the goldfish. The big investment management firms will become increasingly cumbersome, converging on passive investment strategies while more talented managers split off to set up more nimble and entrepreneurial structures.

HEDGE FUND INVESTING AND THE LAW: REGULATION AND REMEDIES

What to watch out for when investing with hedge funds and what redress you may have if you feel that you have had a bad experience with hedge funds.

This chapter has been written with assistance from Bridget Barker, a partner at London lawyers Macfarlanes. Some of the points take a closer look at issues raised in a more general way earlier in the book.

INVESTMENT FREEDOM LEADS TO LOWER RESTRICTIONS

While on the one side, the huge advantage of hedge funds is that they can be structured so that the investment managers/advisors have considerable freedom in investment strategy, this, on the downside, also means that there are usually very few investment restrictions which might safeguard investors' money. Hedge funds, with their risk/reward profiles that are generally higher than those of, for instance, an equity fund, are directed at the more sophisticated investor, not the general public, a group which includes the infamous widows and orphans.

A number of jurisdictions distinguish between the types of funds which are capable of being sold to the public and those which can only be sold to restricted classes of investors, such as non-private investors including expert investors or institutions.

For example, in broad terms, in the EEA, funds which are Ucits (Undertakings for Collective Investments in Transferable Securities) can be sold to the general public, whereas non-Ucits funds (unless they go through a long authorization process) cannot be. In the UK, only funds which have been "recognized" by the Financial Services Authority (FSA) , formerly known as SIB, can be sold to the public – unregulated funds cannot. In the Channel Islands, Jersey and Guernsey, Class 1/A funds can be sold to the public in the UK while others cannot. Hedge funds are most unlikely to fall within the parameters of the Ucits Directive and therefore cannot be recognized by the FSA and so are not capable of being sold to the public in the UK.

WAIVING YOUR RIGHTS

So, in order to be permitted to purchase an interest in a hedge fund, an investor may be requested to agree, or indeed, required to agree, to be treated as an expert or sophisticated investor and waive any rights or remedies which are only available to private investors.

DOCUMENTATION

When acquiring an investment in a hedge fund, it is very important to look carefully at the documentation provided – usually this will be a prospectus or other brochure giving information about the hedge fund and its investment objectives. This will explain how the monies will be invested and give details about the type of securities or other instruments to be acquired. The documentation should also set out any investment restrictions.

> "When acquiring an investment in a hedge fund, it is very important to look carefully at the documentation provided."

WHAT ARE THE IMPORTANT POINTS TO LOOK FOR BEFORE INVESTING?

1. *How is the hedge fund structured?*

Hedge funds come in a number of different guises. Find out whether your proposed hedge fund is:

- a corporate structure which will have limited liability – being either open-ended with a variable share capital or closed-ended with a fixed share capital;

- a unit trust where a trustee will hold the legal title of assets for the benefit of unitholders;
- a limited partnership which, depending on where it is established, may or may not be a separate legal entity and which will normally be fiscally transparent;
- another type of contractual arrangement (e.g., a *fond commun de placement*).

The reason that it is important to find out what type of fund you are thinking of investing in is because, among other things, in an open-ended vehicle, the interests held by investors will be capable of being freely redeemed on a regular basis. However, in a closed-ended fund, the interests will be held by investors throughout the life of the fund and will only be capable of being disposed of during the life of the fund by way of sale, transfer or assignment.

2. *Where is it formed/incorporated? Are there any special points to consider regarding the fund's incorporation? Does the investor have limited liability or is there any possibility that the investor will have to pay up if the hedge funds makes losses?*

3. *What are the charges? Are they clearly set out? Are there entry or front end charges? Are there withdrawal or back end charges?*

4. *How is the performance fee calculated? Does it make sense? Does the investor understand the calculations? Is it fair (or at least properly explained) to investors? When is the performance fee calculated and deducted?*

5. *If the prospectus contains prior performance data – is it fairly presented? Has it been independently checked or audited?*

6. *If the hedge fund can invest in other funds, is the hedge fund suffering charges in the underlying fund (i.e., charges at both levels) or is there a special deal/rebate?*

7. *When can the investor get out? Are there restrictions on redemption?*

8. *Who are the directors; investment managers/advisors; administrators; custodians and sub-custodians? Are they reputable?*

9. *Are the principal players involved in the hedge fund established or operating in a jurisdiction which is regulated or are they subject to any kind of regulatory review? If there is some form of regulation – is it onerous or merely cursory?*

Jersey and Guernsey are considered to be well-regulated, some other offshore islands, less so. The British Virgin Islands have almost no regulation, but are about to bring in a new law which will require funds to be authorized. It is thought that some of the newer financial centres may be trying to attract business and so may be less rigorous in their approaches to regulation and investor protection issues.

10. *Are there any capital adequacy requirements for hedge fund managers or investment advisors, or any formal approval procedures?*

11. *Is the hedge fund established in a jurisdiction where the infrastructure is good and where there is political stability? For instance, could tax suddenly be levied on the hedge fund if the government changes? Is there any possibility that the fund may be forced to restructure or move jurisdiction?*

12. *Is the custodian stable and adequately capitalized? Is the custodian responsible for the acts of any sub-custodians?*

This is a very important point which is frequently overlooked. If a major US bank is appointed custodian, the investor may think all is well, but if the custodian bank then appoints local sub-custodians who are small or under-capitalised or operate under very little regulatory control, then the investor is protected only if the custodian takes responsibility for acts and/or omissions of the sub-custodian. Most banks refuse to accept such responsibility. There is at least one major US custodian bank which will accept liability for the negligence of its sub-custodians but not for their insolvency.

13. *Are the major players responsible to the hedge fund for their negligence, wilful default, bad faith or breach of the particular agreements to which they are a party? What is the level of culpability or have they been appointed without having to take this level of responsibility?*

14. *Who are the core investors? Are they reputable?*

A word here about money laundering. If the hedge fund is used by money launderers there can be very serious consequences. There is now a wide array of regulatory controls designed to stamp out money laundering.

These controls operate at a number of levels. A large number of countries have adopted the Vienna Convention, which is designed to combat drug money laundering, but, regrettably, fewer have implemented the provisions. However, the European Union Directive on the Prevention of Money Laundering in the Financial System has been implemented in all member states. For instance in the UK there are three principal criminal offences aimed at stamping out money laundering. It is an offence to assist a money launderer or to tip-off a money launderer or a third party about an

> **"There is now a wide array of regulatory controls designed to stamp out money laundering."**

investigation or possible investigation into his activities. There is also now a positive obligation under English law to report any suspicion of certain types of money laundering obtained during the course of one's employment, trade or profession. Failure to so report can carry criminal penalties. In addition all persons who carry on investment business in the UK, and certain other activities, are obliged by the provisions of the Money Laundering Regulation 1993 to put in place procedures to verify the identity of clients, keep appropriate records, put in place procedures to combat money laundering and train staff about the law, regulation and internal procedures.

Although some of the offshore centres have not implemented measures which are as far reaching as the UK, investment managers/advisors who are part of an English group may be required to comply with group policy which reflects the UK standards. However, a number of the offshore centres are increasingly concerned that they must be seen to adhere to standards similar to those contained in the European Directive and either have, or are contemplating introducing, legislation to combat money laundering or overseeing the introduction of codes of practice or conduct of business rules. A recent concern is that investors who are trying to evade taxation in their home country may be brought within the provisions of the new regime. In the past, there was a fairly widely held belief that, provided activities did not constitute a crime in the particular jurisdiction, there was no need to make further enquiries. However, if the authorities do widen their approach, the operators of hedge funds may need to be more circumspect before accepting funds from an unknown source.

A fund which the authorities suspect of having "dirty money" in it could face suspension of trading/dealings and freezing of its assets. Any subsequent investigation by the authorities would cause great inconvenience to the investment managers/advisors. There can be a delay in operating the fund in the usual way, as well as the expense and inconvenience of an investigation plus a diversion of management time. The investor could be locked into a fund and be unable to extract his monies during the investigation or work by forensic accountants.

An investigation for money laundering may also attract the unwanted attentions of other regulators and tax authorities.

14. *What return will an investor obtain? How will it be taxed in his hands? Will the hedge fund pay tax on its income/capital or will it pay out gross to investors? Will there be any withholding tax? Will it be possible for the investor or the hedge fund to take advantage of any double tax treaties?* (This is probably only possible for the hedge fund if it is a limited partnership or possibly a unit trust but not if it is a company.)

15. *What law governs the hedge fund documentation? Is it reputable? Would it be difficult to sue?*

If the law is based on a common law system it is unlikely that many of the concepts which apply under English law such as negligence or misrepresentation will be available. However, there may be different forms of redress if the fund has been established under a civil law system or purely under statute. An investor would be well advised to invest in a fund which is operated under a system of law with which he is familiar or otherwise obtain legal advice as to the implications of investing in that particular jurisdiction.

REMEDIES FOR THE INVESTOR

In the event that something goes wrong and the investor loses money, what are his possible remedies?

1. Check selling documents

Has the hedge fund been operated in accordance with the statements in the prospectus?

For example, a prospectus states that the hedge fund's investment objectives are "to seek long term capital growth through investment in a wide range of global equities on major recognized stock markets" and includes the following statements regarding investment limitations:

> In appropriate circumstances, the hedge fund may sell futures and options contracts both to hedge against the risk of market losses on securities held in the portfolio and for speculative purposes. The hedge fund may hold cash, money market securities and floating rate notes or bonds.

If, for example, the hedge fund or its manager incorrectly anticipates a downturn in the prices of equity securities and puts most of the assets of the fund (say 70%) into cash at a time of very low interest rates while global equity markets continue to rise, it is arguable that there has been a misrepresentation in that the hedge fund should be invested in equities when it is actually holding a large proportion of its portfolio in cash.

2. Making a claim

Claims could be available against the hedge fund (or its manager) for misrepresentation, negligence or breach of contact or against the trustee of a unit trust for breach of trust.

(a) Misrepresentation

In common law jurisdictions (which include most of the offshore funds centres which are based on English law, e.g., Bermuda, Cayman, BVI, Jersey, Guernsey and so on) statements contained in selling documents will constitute representations on which an investor will rely when making the decision to invest in the hedge fund. A claim for misrepresentation would require the investor to show that the statements in the selling documents and publicity materials induced him to invest on the basis that the hedge fund would be invested in equities.

A successful claim for misrepresentation entitles the aggrieved party to compensation to put him in the position he would have been in, had the misleading statement never been made. This involves forecasting what would have happened if the investor had never gone into the hedge fund and contrasting it with his position as a result of going into it. In essence, it compensates him for the opportunity cost of investing in the hedge fund, and thus may extend gains forgone by not investing elsewhere.

It would be necessary to show what returns the investor might have expected from another similar fund.

A misrepresentation claim will not compensate the investor for the returns he might have expected from the hedge fund itself if the hedge fund had been operated in accordance with its objectives. It is not a "loss of bargain" claim.

(b) Negligence

A similar difficulty exists with a claim for negligence. The measure of damages is that which is required to put the aggrieved party in the position he would have been in had the negligence not occurred. The aggrieved party is also entitled to compensation for losses flowing from the breach which were "reasonably foreseeable." The investor would have to show that the hedge fund was in breach of a duty of care owed to the investor. A court would have to be convinced that the hedge fund's failure to operate in the way set out (or represented) in the selling documents and its failure to foresee a rise in the market was more than a minor misjudgement, and amounted to a breach of duty of care, and that the fact that the hedge fund did not benefit from the subsequent rise in the market represented a loss which was "reasonably foreseeable."

A more subtle line of argument would be that the hedge fund (or its manager) was negligent in going liquid but not hedging against a possible rise in the market. Acquisition of call options against the appropriate stock index would have offset the gains forgone by the hedge fund as a result of being out of the market.

If the hedge fund had appointed a manager, an investor may have similar claims against the manager if the investor could show that the manager owed the investor a duty of care. If a third party investment advisor had been appointed by the manager, and had advised that the hedge fund should go liquid, then conceivably the investor could make a claim for negligence against the advisor direct. The investor would have to show that the advisor owed him a duty of care. The manager, if sued by the investor, could also bring the investment advisor into the proceedings if he considered that the failure was due to negligent advice from the advisor.

(c) Breach of contract

A claim for breach of contract may be a preferable course for the investor. It would probably be possible to establish that a contract exists between the hedge fund and the investor, under which the fund must operate in accordance with its selling documents or that the manager must operate the fund in such a manner in return for its management fee. The investor would argue that the hedge fund and/or manager was in breach of contract by going 70% liquid. The significant point is that in a claim for breach of contract, the measure of damages is that which would put the aggrieved party in the position he would have been in if the contract had been performed properly. It is essentially forward looking, to where the investor should have been if the contract had been properly performed, not backward looking, to where he would have been had he never invested. Thus there would be a much greater chance of establishing a right to be compensated for gains which the hedge fund did not make because it was out of the market.

(d) Breach of trust

If the vehicle is a unit trust there could also be a claim for breach of trust. Strictly speaking, this brings in principles of equity and equitable remedies, rather than the common law as such. If it is established that the trustee is in breach of its duties, then in addition to the statutory and common law remedies mentioned above, the investor could bring a claim for breach of trust. In principle the trustee must pay restitutory compensation for the actual loss suffered by the trust fund. This extends to all losses incurred before the fund was properly reinvested in accordance with its objectives. The measure of damages may in practice be little different from that for negligence. However, the consequences could be serious for the trustee because there is authority to the effect that the trustee would be liable for losses, regardless of considerations of causation, foreseeability and remoteness of damage.

Against that, the trustee may have some protection under statute, e.g., UK Trustee Act 1926, Section 61, which relieves a trustee from liability for breach of trust if the court is satisfied that the trustee acted honestly and reasonably and ought to be excused (wholly or partly).

3. The law

The laws of the jurisdiction in which the prospectus or other marketing literature was issued or circulated may contain particular provisions which restrict the type of information which may be contained in documents or which make disclosure of certain issues mandatory. If these have not been complied with there may be cause for complaint either as a matter of law or under regulation. For example, under English law, it is a criminal offence to issue a selling document (or investment advertisement) unless it is issued or approved by an authorized person. (See Addendum, page 188.) In addition, if the legal prohibition is breached there is provision under the law that any investment agreement which was entered into as a result of an unauthorized investment advertisement can be set aside and the investor can recover money paid and loss sustained. Therefore if the prospectus is not properly issued the investor can set aside the agreement to purchase shares and recover his money paid for the shares and for his loss of bargain.

In addition there may be a prohibition against cold calling investors. In English law a cold call means a personal visit or oral communication made without express invitation. Consequently, therefore, calls or visits to an investor's home may be prohibited unless they have been specifically agreed to by the investor. Under English law, if there has been a breach of the cold calling laws, an investor may set aside an agreement made in consequence of the cold call and recover the loss of bargain. It may be that a jurisdiction will have particular rules against cold calling. If these have been breached, the investor could look to see if the bargain can be set aside and recover the cost of the investment and possibly loss of profit.

4. Other claims

In certain jurisdictions, the custodian or trustee may have obligations to ensure that the fund manager operates in accordance with selling documents or any applicable regulations. Consequently custodians or trustees must supervise or oversee the operation of the fund in a proper manner and they could be liable to investors if they fail to do so. However, the custodian or trustee may not be under an absolute obligation to prevent, or have direct responsibility for, breaches by the manager. It may simply be obliged to exercise care and diligence to see that no breach occurs. It is therefore possible that the trustee would be able to show that it had made adequate efforts to supervise the manager, but had been unable to control him. If the fund is a limited partnership, the general partner will owe fiduciary duty to other limited partners and if this is breached there may be a cause of action by the limited partners against the general partner.

5. Statutory claims

The law of the jurisdiction under which the fund is established or marketed may contain provisions which would allow an investor to bring a claim under statute. For instance, in the UK Section 62 of the Financial Services Act 1986 (the FSA) gives a statutory right of action to any private investor who suffers loss as a result of a breach of rules and regulations made under the Act. However claims under Section 62 are available to private investors only and not to business or institutional investors.

6. Investors' compensation schemes

It may be that a compensation scheme is operated by the authorities or regulators in the particular jurisdiction. However these are frequently limited in scope and may only reimburse the investor if the hedge fund or its manager becomes insolvent. A compensation scheme may also be further limited in that, for instance it may only cover claims by private investors.

7. Complaints procedure/arbitration/ombudsman

Again the laws or regulations of the jurisdiction in question may offer relief through the medium of an arbitration or ombudsman scheme. Such a scheme may however be limited to relatively small claims. For example the UK's Investors' Compensation Scheme is only able to adjudicate on investors' claims and make awards of up to £100,000 per claim.

8. Complaints to the regulatory authorities

The investor may complain to those in charge, for instance the FSA in the UK or the Financial Services Commission in Guernsey. Can they do anything to help? They may have disciplinary powers which will be used against the operator of the hedge fund but not the power to reimburse investors for any loss they have suffered. The regulators may have the power to fine the manager or withdraw its license to carry on investment business.

9. Auditors

The firm which audits the hedge fund may have a duty to report on the fund although it is not altogether clear whether the duty of the auditors is to the hedge fund itself or to the investors. However this may be an avenue worth pursuing in certain jurisdictions.

10. Fraud

Criminal activity is, of course, prohibited by the criminal law. An investor could see whether this might help bring the offender to justice although it is less likely to produce compensation. For instance, in the UK it is a criminal offence to issue a document which the issuer knows is misleading with a view to inducing persons to acquire shares (Section 47 of the

"The best advice is of course to avoid litigation."

FSA). The investor may be able to bring a prosecution which will result in a fine or imprisonment of an offender but this will not assist him in recovering any money which he has lost.

AVOID LITIGATION – *CAVEAT EMPTOR*

In all jurisdictions, litigation can be expensive, slow and stressful. In this type of case there may be the added problem of proceedings having to be taken abroad and in different time zones, languages or jurisdictions. The best advice is of course to avoid litigation. It therefore becomes all the more important that an investor makes all proper enquiries before he parts with his money and makes an investment.

ADDENDUM:

NOTES ON THE FINANCIAL SERVICES ACT 1986,

SECTION 57

1. The restriction

Section 57 of the Act prohibits any person other than an authorised person (most obviously a member of a Self-Regulating Organisation such as SFA or IMRO) from issuing or causing to be issued an investment advertisement in the United Kingdom, unless that investment advertisement has been approved by an authorised person. Breach of Section 57 is a criminal offence. In addition any investment agreement relating to the investment which was the subject of the advertisement, entered into after issue of the investment advertisement will be unenforceable at the option of the investor unless a court decides that the investor was not influenced to a material extent by the advertisement in making his decision to enter into the agreement or that the advertisement was not misleading and fairly stated the risks involved. Unless the court otherwise decides an investor will be entitled to recover any money and property paid or transferred by him together with compensation for any loss sustained by him.

An "investment advertisement" is an advertisement which either:

- invites persons to enter into, or offer to enter into, an investment agreement or exercise rights conferred by an investment, acquire, dispose of, underwrite or convert the investment or
- contains information calculated to lead directly or indirectly to persons doing so.

Dealing with each element in turn:

a. Advertisement is widely, and not exhaustively, defined to mean any advertisement including (without setting out the full list) notices, signs, circulars, catalogues, pictures, radio or television broadcasts and advertisements disseminated in any other manner. The definition is accordingly capable not only of encompassing letters and other documents, as well as electronic means of advertising, but also oral communications. Information which is made available on the Internet system is capable of constituting an investment advertisement. The consensus is that a scripted "road show" selling investment products or presenting a share issue to analysts will be an advertisement and there is some suggestion that even unscripted responses to an interview may do so. While, in view of the sanctions for breaching Section 57, there is no room for complacency, it should be borne in mind that the definition commences with the phrase "Every form of advertising" without defining "advertisement" or "advertise", and it is hoped that the courts will seek to give those words their normally accepted meanings.

b. The advertisement must invite individuals to enter into or offer to enter into investment agreements. ("Investment agreement" is widely defined, and for practical purposes should be taken to include all securities transactions.) An example of an invitation to potential investors to enter into an investment agreement would be a prospectus for a hedge fund.

c. Alternatively, the advertisement must be "calculated to lead, directly or indirectly" to persons entering into investment agreements. This is more difficult and in particular relevant in relation to brochures or other selling documents which are used by fund operators.

i) What is meant by calculated? The better view is that this does not require an intention on the part of the issuer that the effect should be achieved, but rather that the effect should be likely in the circumstances, so it is an objective test. There is a concern that any advertisement which gives information regarding a fund (including its report and accounts) may influence a decision to buy or sell shares. Accordingly, depending on the nature of the information, it may be calculated to lead to a purchase or a sale.

ii) Directly or indirectly. The information in the investment advertisement may be one of a number of factors which causes a person to buy or sell shares, and in that sense it may be said to have an indirect effect, but there must be a point at which the materiality of the information to the investment decision is so low that it can no longer be said to have led to the decision. The phrase also leads to difficulties where an investor subscribes for or buys shares on the back of a formal document such as a prospectus having previously received some form of brochure or other introductory or warm-up materials. There may be an argument for saying that the brochure is not an investment advertisement because the investment decision is taken solely on the basis of the formal prospectus which sets out the full terms. Yet the idea that the formal prospectus effectively supersedes the brochure is weakened by the use of the word "indirectly".

HEDGE FUNDS: THE FUTURE

What does the future hold for this exciting branch of investment? How will the industry grow and what new developments can investors expect? Will hedge funds become easier to access?

WHY DO PEOPLE INVEST?

Why do most people – private investors – save or invest their money? Certainly a large part of the reason must be to ensure financial security for themselves and future generations. The biggest pot of investment money out there in the investment markets is pension money. Whether it's part of a huge pot of State pension funding, deducted at source from the wages of ordinary people, or part of a private trust of money put together by more wealthy people, it's there to be invested to provide financial security for the future.

This money is known by alternative investment managers – whether they are the hedge fund managers, the managed futures managers or those who invest in commodities or foreign exchange – as institutional investment funds and it is this money that they hope to attract into their fund products or investment programs.

> "Traditionally, institutional money has been invested in a very risk-averse way."

Traditionally, institutional money has been invested in a very risk-averse way, but this is changing. And when the board of a conservative institution decides to invest with a specialist manager, it tends to commit a serious amount of money which partly reflects the size of the assets it has at its disposal. An institution also tends to keep its investments with a chosen manager for some time. Having made the commitment of investing with a manager, it is prepared to stick it out through good and bad periods of returns.

This is the sort of investment that investment managers like. They are dealing with professionals, they are dealing with people who understand that investment returns can come and go over the short term, and they are dealing with people who can afford to look to the longer term.

AN AGING POPULATION

The reason that traditionally risk-averse institutional investment managers are looking towards the alternative investment management sector is that the people who are responsible for investing the bulk of institutional money – the pension managers – have a problem. The Western world, has an aging population. The World Bank recently referred to this as the "biggest problem of our time" in its report *Averting the Old Age Crisis*.

An aging population means that while formerly pension funds provided by the State had surpluses, and then, once those were used up, had enough working population to fund the retired population, these days there are not enough earners to fund the non-earners. The delicate balance between the two types of population has been lost. And this is the pattern across the Western world. The result is greater pressure on governments and private pension providers to achieve higher investment returns on the money that they obtain.

Throughout Europe, most pension fund assets are still invested in bonds rather than equities. The exception is the UK where about 80% of a typical fund's assets are invested in equities. Debbie Harrison, writing in *Pension Provision and Fund Management In Europe* published by FT Financial Publishing says:

> Governments have already started to relax investment restraints but it is a slow process and the bond mentality in continental Europe is just as embedded as the equity mentality in the UK. However, as a general observation it seems clear that funds will push for greater investment freedom as they seek to improve returns and/or reduce costs. The main asset classes to benefit will be domestic and foreign equities and, to a lesser extent, foreign bonds. As equity investment gains in popularity, clearly there will be a corresponding increase in the number of foreign equity specialist appointments, particularly where the domestic stock market is limited in size and scope compared with the size of pension fund assets. This trend is already well under way with leading pan-European managers regularly gaining new mandates, although domestic equity and bond portfolios are expected to remain with local managers. Passive investment and active quantitative techniques have a strong

appeal to some of the larger pension funds in Europe, due, so the managers claim, to the disciplined approach, the more predictable results and the fact that the success of the venture does not rely on a star manager who, likely as not, will be poached by a rival before the year is out.

Which is all good news for the hedge fund industry. The picture seems to be that as pressure mounts on governments to ensure adequate pension provision, pension providers will look to a wider variety of types of investment to raise returns. While it's a long jump from looking at just bonds to looking at equities as well and then to hedge funds – it's a step in that direction.

A report published by the European Federation of Retirement Provision entitled *European Pension Funds: Their Impact on European Capital Markets and Competitiveness* produced the following key points for the pension industry:

1. The long-term nature of pension fund investments ought to be a prime consideration of the regulatory and supervisory system.
2. If pension funds move to their specific ideal asset allocation by applying asset liability management, this implies in general that they should hold more real assets – that is, equities and real estate. This in turn will result in short term fluctuations and volatility in asset prices.
3. The supervisory authorities should encourage a long term approach by examining funds' solvency, not only on an annual basis, which would accentuate short termism, but also over five and 10 year rolling periods. This would support the long term investment horizon of such funds.
4. Freedom of investment requires a high level of control by all those in charge of running pensions funds and it needs to be balanced with appropriate supervision.
5. Regulation has to be clear and must support the objectives of the pension funds. Any interference in the asset allocation process is likely to result in suboptimal returns and increased risk.
6. A "prudent man" rule should be generally applied to investments.
7. The tax status of pension funds should be improved in a majority of member states so that it is an incentive, rather than a disincentive, towards funding and the optimization of investment returns. The tax authorities will benefit from this change due to the increased tax

receipts on payment of benefits. Retired people drawing a pension represent the fastest growing segment of the overall population.

8. Progress must be made with the co-ordination of taxation to promote pan-EU mobility of labour and pension rights, otherwise Europe may jeopardize basic Treaty rights.

Debbie Harrison, *Pension Provision and Fund Management in Europe*

THE US STORY

The institutionalization of hedge funds and other types of alternative investment is already happening to some extent in the US. December 1997's *MAR/Hedge* reports that while in 1970 Yale University had no allocation to absolute return strategies, today, they allocate 20% to such strategies and, overall, Yale has 50% invested with non-traditional strategies. "Institutional consultants are now including hedge funds as an investment category" says Lois Peltz, writing in the December 1997 issue.

Speaking as the keynote speaker at *MAR/Hedge*'s fourth Bermuda conference, Richard Elden of Grosvenor Capital Management predicted that the next 20–30 years will see as many changes in the hedge fund industry as have happened in the last 20–30 years. Elden believes that by 2020, the size of the hedge fund universe could be considerably bigger than that of the current mutual fund industry. He sees the funds of the future as very integrated, mixing traditional and non-traditional funds, active and passive investment together in a large investment cocktail.

> "The institutionalization of hedge funds and other types of alternative investment is already happening to some extent in the US."

The argument in favor of hedge funds is very simple. Previous chapters of this book show academic and commercial evidence that hedge funds can provide consistently higher returns than more passively managed funds, and the good ones combine this with lower volatility and low correlation with other investment sectors: the dream combination for any investor, institutional or otherwise, one would think.

THE UPS AND THE DOWNS

Writing this book during the second half of 1997, I have been constantly nervous that shortly after it was finished and on the way to being printed there would be a huge market crash which would affect what I say now about hedge funds in adverse market conditions. The markets have been kind to me, as it happens. We have had a few mini-dramas in the stockmarkets in the US, Europe and the Far East over October – enough of a downturn to see what happens to the alternative investment community in volatile and dropping markets. Anyone can make money during the bull market run that we have seen over the past few years – but achieving in a climate of market volatility is the clever thing.

DISPELLING A MYTH

The most famous of the "hedge fund" collapses in October 1997 came with the severe losses at Niederhoffer Investments. There was much gleeful press coverage of this firm's loss of more than $60m in one day but most coverage failed to notice that Niederhoffer Investments is a futures fund, not a hedge fund. The losses came from a duff derivatives position – specifically a $50m margin call on a large short position on S&P puts, according to MAR. The S&P went down 554 points on October 27 and Victor Niederhoffer ended the week out of business.

The investment performance of Niederhoffer's range of funds – some hedge and some futures – has been tracked by MAR since 1987. Since then he had a compound annualized return of 20% and had made double digit returns every year between 1987 and 1996, except for 1992 when he lost 10%. However, behind those returns lies a history of volatility – one night in 1994 saw Niederhoffer lose 25% on the Japanese yen only to return to near level by the end of the month.

The bad publicity surrounding the Niederhoffer collapse demonstrates my point made in the opening chapter that hedge funds need

197

to be separated from futures funds. The looseness of the definition of hedge funds rebounds against them. The type and the speed of losses such as those experienced by Niederhoffer are peculiar to derivatives trading – and highly leveraged trading at that. The looseness of the definition rebounds when futures funds and all the negative publicity that surrounds derivatives and derivative losses gets lumped in with the hedge fund arena.

Hedge funds do suffer collapses but it tends to take longer. Hedge funds' positions tend to be more complicated and take longer to unravel – the Askin collapse with a loss of $600m on mortgage securities and their derivatives took six weeks and caused knock-on effects in the mortgage securities markets for the best part of a year.

The volatility of October 1997 saw a mixture of reactions from hedge funds. According to data from *MAR/Hedge* 74.2% outperformed the S&P. Of the 783 funds reporting to the *MAR/Hedge* database in October 1997 about 45% had a positive month with one fund, Anomalous Partners – a long/short fund – achieving returns of 44% over the month and 17 other funds achieving double digit gains. The greatest earners were the short funds – poised for just such a market scenario they achieved a median 3% over the month – while the next best, market neutral funds had a median gain of 1%.

Hedge funds based on emerging markets had a tough time with the volatility – unsurprising when one considers that much of the downturn was caused by problems in the Far East markets. Problems in the emerging markets tend to affect the other emerging markets of Eastern Europe and Latin America. Of the 48 emerging markets funds reporting to *MAR/Hedge* that had losses greater than 10%, 17 were regional emerging market funds.

Managed futures funds suffered across the board in October 1997 with the MAR Trading Advisor Qualified Universe Index showing a loss of 0.5% and the MAR Fund/Pool Qualified Universe Index showing a loss of 1.8%. The discretionary advisors achieved the best performance with a gain of 0.8% against the performance of systematic traders who dropped 1.6%.

The managed futures industry saw an enormous growth in the late 1980s based largely on the fact that it appeared to have attained the achievement of non-correlation with the equity and bond markets. Stories abounded of leading managed futures funds which achieved significant returns during the market crash of 1987 and the managed futures industry's marketing managers dined out on these tales for many years. David McCarthy of GAM speaking at the *MAR/Hedge* Bermuda conference in 1997 on "Myth and Illusion: The Search for Non-Correlated Strategies" concluded that there was no such thing as a truly market neutral or market independent investment strategy. He said, wryly, that the only thing that rose in a bear market was correlation and, in the long term, it appears that he is right. Managed futures funds have failed to sustain their purple patch – since the early 1990s performance has been dull and returns erratic with only a few stars, such as John Henry or Robert Tamiso showing good, consistent results.

> **"The hedge fund sector has grown successfully this far through rising above the more esoteric investment styles."**

Hedge funds need to be aware that marketing themselves as a clever, indeed non-correlating, alternative to traditional investment is a very dangerous path to follow. The hedge fund sector has grown successfully this far through rising above the more esoteric investment styles and remaining attached to the mainstream. Hedge fund managers are from the mainstream of investment – they are just more specialized. If they can remain in the core of the institutional investment management arena, they will grow in size.

You want to invest in hedge funds because they invest in things you understand but they do it with more skill than you could. That is the strength of the sector.

PREDICTING THE FUTURE

- Hedge funds will become more available to the smaller investor – minimum investments will come down, perhaps through increased growth in the consultancy and fund of funds industry.
- Retail funds will respond to the challenge of hedge funds moving into their market by increasingly offering access to more specialized

investment. This has already happened to a limited extent by the offer of emerging market funds to investors by the mainstream retail fund management companies.

- As hedge funds get bigger, their fees will come down.
- As hedge funds become, in some cases, more retail-oriented, their disclosure practices and registrations will become less obscure.
- Institutional funds, desperate for better returns, will use specialist investment managers more.
- More other types of managers will pretend to be hedge funds.
- Unless hedge funds take a new name, they will continue to be confused with derivatives and futures funds and get a bad press.
- Hedge fund managers who cannot control volatility will lose money under management.
- Hedge fund managers who under perform will lose money under management.
- Huge hedge fund managers who have large amounts of money under management will either give money back to their investors or split their investment management into different parts.
- More talented investment managers will leave large institutions to set up hedge funds.
- New regulatory bodies, designed specifically to oversee the activities of hedge funds, will come into being, bringing with them a new raft of regulation.

BIBLIOGRAPHY

Against the Gods – The Remarkable Story of Risk by Peter L Bernstein, published by John Wiley & Sons Inc.

Managed Futures – An Investor's Guide by Beverly Chandler, published by John Wiley & Sons Ltd.

Hedge Funds and Managed Futures by Dr Philipp Cottier, published by Paul Haupt.

Hedge Funds – An Introduction to Skill-Based Investment Strategies by Richard Hills, published by Rushmere Wynn.

Evaluating and Implementing Hedge Fund Strategies edited by Ronald A Lake, published by Euromoney Books.

The Alchemy of Finance by George Soros, published by John Wiley & Sons Inc.

GLOSSARY OF TERMS

Absolute returns Performance returns that are measured independently of a benchmark or index.

Alpha The non-systematic risk element of a portfolio. *MAR/Hedge* quotes alpha as the expected rate of return for the hedge fund manager when the rate of return for the specified benchmark is zero. This static measure reflects the value of the investment relative to the index at an instant in time.

Arbitrage Profiting from a price difference between securities in the same or different markets.

Beta A measure of price movement, risk or volatility, relative to the specified benchmark. *MAR/Hedge* quotes beta as representing the change in return for every 1% change in the index. If the beta is more than 1, the investment typically gains or loses more than the index. In mathematical terms, beta measures the slope of the curve that portrays the investment's performance.

Benchmark A reference security or index which allows a comparison and evaluation of the performance of an investment. Effective benchmarks have similar risk/return characteristics to the investments with which they are being compared.

Bottom-up stock-picking Investment managers who choose stocks through fundamental analysis of each company.

Commodity Trading Advisor (CTA) A person or company who analyses or trades in the derivative markets.

Derivatives Derivatives are financial instruments which derive from underlying securities, e.g., futures based on equities or commodities.

Downside deviation A risk measure which takes into account all the instances where an investment yields less than a specified target rate.

Drawdown A loss during a given period.

Efficient frontier The efficient frontier is a curve which describes the optimal combination of a portfolio of assets to achieve return, with the least amount of risk.

Futures An agreement to purchase or sell a certain amount of a certain commodity at a time and place specified at the outset at a price which is agreed at the outset.

Fund of funds A fund whose business it is to invest in a wide range of other funds.

Gearing Also known as leverage: this is the relationship between assets and their exposure in the market. It is usually stated as a percentage, two times is 200% gearing.

Hedge fund An absolute return investment fund designed to invest in a wide range of instruments in order to achieve a high return for a given level of risk. It is usually based offshore and the manager is reimbursed through an incentive fee.

Hedging A process through which the risk of loss due to adverse price movements is transferred.

Limited partnership A US vehicle for a collection of partners in a partnership which consists of 99 partners and one managing partner.

Long only manager A manager who holds positive assets.

Long position Holding a positive amount of an asset.

Macro Investment strategies based on major economic issues.

Micro Investment strategies based on issues specific to an individual country, company or sector.

NAV Net asset value: the assets of a fund minus its liabilities.

Prime broker The prime broker looks after the back office functions of clearing, settlement and custody for a fund, plus it undertakes the shorting and leverage activities.

Sharpe ratio An annualised measure of the return above the risk-free rate per unit of return variability. The formula is the annualised geometric rate of return minus rate of return on a risk-free investment divided by the annualised arithmetic standard deviation.

Sortino ratio An annualised measure of the amount of return above the target rate per unit of downside risk.

Standard deviation The standard deviation of a numerical series is a measure of the extent to which numerical values in the series differ from the arithmetic mean.

Top-down stock-picker This is a method of investing in which the investment manager invests according to macro strategies.

INDEX